Favourite Character Cakes

Debbie Brown

Favourite Character Cakes

Debbie Brown

KÖNEMANN

DEDICATION

To Dawn and Jackie,
close sisters, best friends

First published 1997 by Merehurst
Limited
Reprinted 1997
Ferry House, 51–57 Lacy Road, Putney,
London SW15 1PR
Design: Anita Ruddell
Photography by Clive Streeter

© 1999 for the English text
Könemann Verlagsgesellschaft mbH
Bonner Straße 126, D-50968 Köln
Production Manager: Detlev Schaper
Assistant: Nicola Leurs
Reproductions: Reproservice Werner Pees
Printing and binding: Sing Cheong
Printing Ltd., Hong Kong
Printed in Hong Kong, China
ISBN 3-8290-1480-5
10 9 8 7 6 5 4 3 2 1

MR.MEN   LITTLE MISS

Contents

Introduction

THE CAKES in this collection are inspired by some of the most popular and classic characters from children's fiction, television and greetings cards. Every child has his or her favourite, but all the cakes in this book will appeal to youngsters of all ages, as well as to many adults.

Children's eyes always light up when the birthday cake is brought in, but if the cake also looks like one of their favourite characters, their delight is doubled, especially if the cake is the triumphant finale of a birthday tea whose theme has been based on that same character.

One of the aspects of character cakes that makes them so appealing to children is the brightly coloured pastes and icings used to decorate them. For those who are concerned about colour content, there are a number of projects in the book that use techniques designed to cut down on the amount of colouring used. For example, the red of Postman Pat's van is painted on to white sugarpaste using diluted food colouring paste rather than coating the cake with red sugarpaste. Read the instructions carefully before deciding which project you wish to make.

Each cake in this book is large enough for the average birthday party, although some have been made with slightly smaller celebrations in mind.

Have fun!

Basic Recipes

For successful results, use these simple basic recipes that are suitable for making any of the character cakes in this book.

MADEIRA SPONGE CAKE

The secret of successful novelty cake-making is to start with a firm, moist cake which will withstand any cutting and shaping required without crumbling. A Madeira recipe is a good choice and can be flavoured to give variety.

To make a Madeira cake suitable for any of the designs in this book, first grease and line the required bakeware (see the chart on pages 84–85), then proceed as follows:

1 Preheat the oven to 160°C (325°F) Gas 3. Sift the two types of flour together into a bowl.

2 Put the butter or soft margarine and caster (superfine) sugar together in a large mixing bowl, and beat until the mixture is pale and fluffy.

3 Gradually add the eggs, one at a time, with a spoonful of the sifted flour, beating well after each addition. Beat in any flavouring required (see suggestions, right).

4 Fold the remaining flour into the mixture.

5 Spoon the mixture into the bakeware. Make a dip in the top with the back of the spoon.

6 Bake in the centre of the oven until a skewer inserted in the centre comes out clean (see chart for approximate time).

7 Leave to cool for 5 minutes, then turn out on to a wire rack and leave to cool completely. When cold, store in an airtight container until ready to use.

Flavourings

Vanilla Add 1 teaspoon vanilla essence to every 6-egg mixture.
Lemon Add the grated rind and/or juice of 1 lemon to every 6-egg mixture.
Chocolate Mix 2–3 tablespoons unsweetened cocoa powder with 1 tablespoon milk to every 6-egg mixture.
Almond Add 1 teaspoon almond essence and 2–3 tablespoons of ground almonds to every 6-egg mixture.

SUGARPASTE

For convenience, use ready-made sugarpaste (rolled fondant) which is of high quality and easily available from supermarkets and cake decorating suppliers.

BUTTERCREAM

As well as forming a filling between layers of cake, a thin coat of buttercream spread on the cake will fill any small gaps and provide a smooth surface on which to apply the sugarpaste (rolled fondant). Buttercream can also be flavoured.

Makes about 500g (1lb)
125g (4oz/½ cup) butter, softened, or soft margarine
1 tablespoon milk
375g (12oz/2½ cups) icing (confectioners') sugar, sifted

1 Put the butter or soft margarine in a bowl.

2 Add the milk and any flavouring (see page 9).

3 Sift the icing sugar into the bowl, a little at a time, beating well after each addition, until all the sugar is incorporated and the buttercream has a light, creamy texture.

4 Store the buttercream in an airtight container until required.

Flavourings

Vanilla Add 1 teaspoon vanilla essence.
Lemon Replace the milk with fresh or concentrated lemon juice.
Chocolate Mix the milk and 2 tablespoons unsweetened cocoa powder to a paste and add to the mixture.
Coffee Mix the milk and 1 tablespoon instant coffee powder to a paste and add to the mixture.

ROYAL ICING

Makes about 280g (9oz)
1 egg white
250–280g (8–9oz/1¾ cups) icing
(confectioners') sugar, sifted

1 Put the egg white in a bowl. Beat in the icing sugar, a little at a time, until the icing is firm and glossy, and forms peaks when the spoon is pulled out.

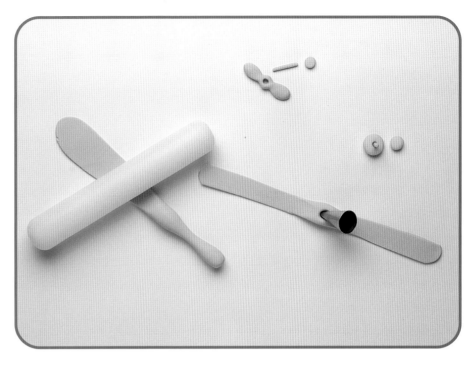

2 Cover the bowl with a damp cloth for a few minutes before use.

PASTILLAGE

This paste dries extremely hard, very quickly. It will not bend or lose its shape and is most suitable for precision work, such as for making rotor-blades for Budgie The Little Helicopter (see page 38).

When using pastillage, you have to work quite quickly as it forms a crust soon after being exposed to the air. It is therefore unsuitable for modelling, unless you mix it 50/50 with sugarpaste (rolled fondant).

Pastillage can be obtained in high-quality powder form from cake decorating suppliers, but the recipe below is very simple.

Makes about 375g (12oz)
1 egg white
345g (11oz/2¼ cups) icing
(confectioners') sugar, sifted
2 teaspoons gum tragacanth

1 Put the egg white in a bowl and add 280g (9oz) icing sugar a little at a time, mixing well after each addition.

2 Sprinkle the gum tragacanth over the top and put aside for 10 minutes.

3 Turn the mixture out on to a surface and knead in the remaining icing sugar.

4 Double wrap in polythene or cling-film (plastic wrap) and store in an airtight container until required.

pastillage or modelling paste, both of which have a gum additive, with egg white.

To stick sugar items together, you need only slightly dampen the paste surface with sugar glue, using a fine paintbrush. If you apply too much, your modelled piece may slide out of place. Gently press in position, holding for a few moments. Small pieces of foam sponge can be used to support glued modelled pieces until dry, if necessary.

MODELLING PASTE

Modelling paste is sugarpaste (rolled fondant) with a gum additive. When the gum is incorporated, it makes the paste firm but pliable so it is easier to work with. Items modelled from modelling paste will dry harder and also keep their shape.

A natural gum called gum tragacanth, which is widely used in the food industry, is usually used to make modelling paste. A man-made alternative called carboxy methyl cellulose (CMC) is cheaper than gum tragacanth and also goes further.

However, if you do not want to make your own modelling paste before embarking on the projects in this book, there are some ready-made modelling pastes available that give good results. Even more useful, they can be obtained pre-coloured.

All items are available from cake decorating suppliers.

Makes about 500g (1lb)
2 teaspoons gum tragacanth
500g (1lb) sugarpaste (rolled fondant)

Put the gum tragacanth on a work surface and knead it into the sugarpaste. Double wrap the modelling paste in polythene or clingfilm (plastic wrap) and store in an airtight container for at least an hour before use.

SUGAR GLUE

All the cake designs in this book depend on sugar glue to stick the components together. An edible glue can be made in a variety of ways, depending on what ingredients are to hand.

Cool boiled water will stick sugar together, but is not strong enough for all modelled pieces. Egg white is a good edible glue, as is royal icing, or a mixture of any paste diluted with a few drops of water. To make an extra-strong glue, mix

Techniques

PAINTING ON SUGAR

Colour strengths

You can dilute food colouring pastes with clear alcohol (gin or vodka) in preference to water as alcohol evaporates more quickly. The strength of the colour depends on the dilution. For a pale water-colour effect, only a tiny amount of colour should be added to the alcohol or water. For a strong colour, add more food colouring.

When painting on sugar, the brush should be kept quite dry to avoid the

paint running or even the sugar melting. Blot excess liquid from the paintbrush using a dry cloth or some absorbent kitchen paper. If a strong solid colour dries a little streaky, apply a second coat.

Mixing colours

To vary a colour slightly and give a different hue, you can add minute amounts of different colours from the neighbouring colours on the colour wheel. If you are nervous about mixing your own colours, use different shades of the same colour from the vast range of food colouring pastes available.

Patterns

Patterns like the check design on the Forever Friends sofa (page 42) are painted in stages with brush strokes in one direction first, left to dry a little, then finished with brush strokes in the opposite direction.

Water-colour effects

The water-colour effects on the sides of the Beatrix Potter cake (page 76), and the models of Peter Rabbit and his friends, are built up gradually, painting the background through to the foreground. A wash of very pale colour should be painted on first and left to dry. Next, a slightly stronger dilution of colour is used to paint in the detail. If you are nervous about painting on a cake, practise on a plain sheet of paper first. Remember, any painted mistakes on sugar can be removed with a damp cloth.

Woodgrain

To create a woodgrain effect, painted brushstrokes will suffice on something small. For a larger area, scratch uneven lines over the surface with a knife or cocktail stick (toothpick) to give the texture of wood, then paint on diluted food colouring. As the diluted food colouring is brushed over the surface, the colour will run into the scratches, giving an appearance of wood. Firm bristle paintbrushes are good to use as they work over the surface quickly; these can be obtained very cheaply from toyshops.

For a quick woodgrain effect without painting, colour the paste brown and scratch lines over the surface as in The Smurfs (page 62).

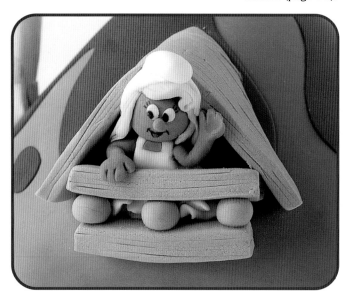

Stippling

Stippling food colouring on to paste is a simple, effective and controllable method of adding colour. Preferably use a medium-sized, firm bristle paintbrush and only collect a little diluted food colouring on to the tip. Blot excess liquid off the brush with a cloth or absorbent kitchen paper, then repeatedly dot over the surface of the paste, keeping the paintbrush vertical.

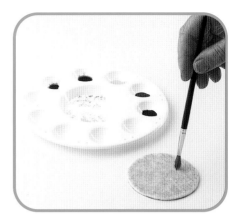

SUGAR STICKS

Sugar supports for models can be made from leftover pastillage or modelling paste. Roll thin sticks of paste in different lengths and leave to dry thoroughly before use. To support your modelled figures, insert the sugar stick down into the body, then gently push on the head, using sugar glue to secure. An alternative to sugar stick supports is to use lengths of raw dried spaghetti.

Never use cocktail sticks (toothpicks) as supports; they are sharp and could cause injury.

CREATING TEXTURE

Fur

When modelling animals, an impression of fur can be achieved by scratching lines over the surface of the modelling paste with a cocktail stick (toothpick). For something more detailed, however, royal icing can be used to create a variety of textures. When piping texture, the royal icing should be firm enough to keep its shape after application. If it is too soft, the royal icing will slowly run.

For Old Bear and Little Bear (page 58) the basic shapes of the bears are made from modelling paste and left to dry. For the rough, slightly bare look of Old Bear, the royal icing is applied without a piping tube (tip). Cut or tear a small hole in the tip of the piping bag and apply the royal icing, working in the direction the fur would grow. For Little Bear's curly fur, use a medium plain piping tube and pipe balls of royal icing next to each other over the surface.

Grass

Lines marked over the surface of sugarpaste with a knife give a quick grass effect. More realistic-looking grass can be obtained by pressing the tip of a star piping tube (tip) repeatedly into soft sugarpaste. Bear in mind that wind blows blades of grass in different directions, so press the tube in at different angles.

BETTY BOOP ™

The cartoon character Betty Boop is well known as the singing and dancing flapper, and for those immortal words 'boop-oop-a-doop'.

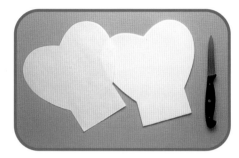

BACK-DROP

1 Make a card template of the back-drop (see page 88). Roll out the pastillage and cut out the back-drop, using the template. Put aside to dry completely, turning once to dry both sides.

CAKE

2 Colour 375g (12oz) sugarpaste red. Roll out and use to cover the cake board. Trim the crust from the cake and slice 3.5cm (1½ inches) from the point. Cut a layer in the cake, then sandwich back together using buttercream. Spread a thin layer of buttercream over the surface of the cake to help the sugarpaste stick.

3 Roll out 500g (1lb) sugarpaste and cover the cake completely, trimming excess from around the base. Position the cake on the cake board. Pipe a snail's trail around the base of the cake and

around the edge of the pastillage back-drop using royal icing and a no. 2 piping tube. Make card templates for the medium and small hearts (see page 88). Colour 100g (3½oz) modelling paste red and roll out thinly. Using the templates, cut out two of each. When dry, stick in position using a little sugar glue. Reserve the red trimmings.

MATERIALS

20cm (8 inch) heart-shaped cake (page 85)
25cm (10 inch) heart-shaped cake board
125g (4oz) pastillage
875g (1¾lb) sugarpaste (rolled fondant)
315g (10oz) buttercream
185g (6oz) royal icing
185g (6oz) modelling paste
red, flesh, black, yellow and blue food colouring pastes
clear alcohol (gin or vodka) or cool boiled water
sugar glue
ribbon trimming

☆

EQUIPMENT

card for templates
large rolling pin
sharp knife
greaseproof paper piping bags
no. 2 plain piping tube (tip)
sharp, pointed scissors
fine paintbrush

6 Using royal icing to secure, assemble Betty Boop on the pastillage back-drop. Stick her legs in place first, making sure that when the back-drop is in position, her shoes just sit on top of the cake. Lay the pastillage back-drop back down, and then stick the remaining pieces in position. Dilute a little black food colouring paste with clear alcohol and paint Betty Boop's hair, eyes, eyebrows, shoes and garter using a fine paintbrush. Paint a little diluted blue on to her eyes. Stick the ribbon trim around the base of the cake.

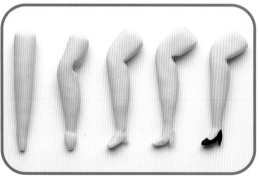

BETTY BOOP

4 Colour 45g (1½oz) modelling paste flesh coloured. Using the photograph (above) as a guide, make Betty Boop's legs first using 7g (¼oz) flesh-coloured paste for each.

5 Model Betty Boop's heart-shaped head using 22g (¾oz) flesh-coloured modelling paste. Snip her hair curls using the tip of a pair of scissors, and curl up. Colour 15g (½oz) modelling paste black and make her dress, hollowing out the base to fit over her legs. With the remaining flesh-coloured paste, model her arms, shoulders and hands in one piece, and stick in position on her dress. Model her tiny nose. Make two tiny circles for her eyes using a minute piece of white modelling paste. Using the red trimmings, make her lips and a tiny heart for her garter. Colour the remaining modelling paste yellow and make her bangles and earrings.

TO FINISH

7 When everything is completely dry, secure the back-drop in position using the remaining royal icing.

Sooty™

Sooty and Sweep – television's favourite glove puppets – have been entertaining generations of children for over 40 years. In 1964 Soo joined them and, more recently, little cousin Scampi became the fourth member of the gang.

BOARD

1 Roll out 440g (14oz) sugarpaste and use to cover the cake board. Using a 20cm (8 inch) circle template and star cutters, indent the spotlight circle, slightly off-centre, and all the stars in the sugarpaste. Dilute some yellow and black food colouring paste with a little clear alcohol and paint the board. Put aside to dry.

TABLE

2 Trim the crust from the cake. Cut the cake in half, then in half again to make four squares. Sandwich the squares, one on top of the other, using buttercream, then spread a thin layer of buttercream over the surface of the cake to help the sugarpaste stick. Roll out 440g (14oz) sugarpaste and cut out pieces to fit each side and the top of the cake. Position the cake on the cake board. Paint a little diluted yellow food colouring around the base of the cake only.

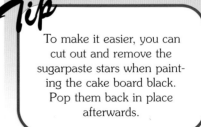

Tip

To make it easier, you can cut out and remove the sugarpaste stars when painting the cake board black. Pop them back in place afterwards.

SOOTY

3 Colour 170g (5½oz) modelling paste yellow. Roll 75g (2½oz) into a fat teardrop shape for Sooty's body. Model his two legs using 22g (¾oz) paste, indenting the lines on his feet with a knife. Using a further 22g (¾oz) paste, roll two sausage shapes for his arms and bend in the middle. Put a minute piece of yellow modelling paste aside for Scampi's hat initial. Use the remaining yellow paste to model Sooty's head by rolling a ball, then indenting slightly for the eyes and shaping his muzzle. Stick Sooty's head on to his body and stick his legs in place using a little sugar glue. Colour 45g (1½oz) modelling paste red. Thinly roll out 30g (1oz) and cut an oblong for Sooty's dunga- rees, at least 6x18cm (2½x7 inches). Wrap around Sooty's tummy, smoothing and trim- ming around his legs, then smooth around the back. Trim away excess and smooth the join closed. Stick Sooty's arms in

place using a little sugar glue. Cut out two dungaree straps and two turn-ups using the trimmings, and stick in place. Colour a minute piece of modelling paste blue and make two buttons.

SOO, SWEEP & SCAMPI

4 To make Soo, take a 45g (1½oz) piece of modelling paste. Separate off a small piece and model into a ball. Flatten to make Soo's neck. Roll the remaining piece into a ball, indent for Soo's eyes and shape a muzzle, keeping her cheeks full. Push in the end of a paintbrush to indent her mouth, then mark her smile with a cocktail stick. To make Sweep, colour 45g (1½ oz) modelling paste grey. Model Sweep's head, making it narrower at the top and shaping the muzzle. Push in the end of a paintbrush to open his mouth. Using a little of the remaining red modelling paste, make Soo's bow and Sweep's collar. To make Scampi, colour 30g (1oz) modelling paste golden brown and model his head, indenting his mouth as before. Colour 7g (¼ oz) modelling paste dark blue and make Scampi's hat and tie. Colour 45g (1½ oz) modelling paste black. Using 7g (¼ oz), make ears for Soo, Sweep and Scampi. Using 7g (¼ oz) white modelling paste, make Scampi's collar and roll a long sausage shape for Sooty's magic wand, cutting the ends straight. Paint the wand with diluted black food colouring, and leave to dry.

TO FINISH

5 Assemble Soo, Sweep and Scampi at the base of the cake, sticking them in position with a little sugar glue. With the remaining black and red modelling paste, make Sooty's ears, Soo's eye patches and all the eyes, eyebrows, noses and vertical lines beneath the noses, sticking in place with sugar glue. Stick minute pieces of white paste on to each eye to highlight. Make the red stripes for Scampi's tie and cut a triangle for his hat. Model his initial using the remaining yellow modelling paste. Split 7g (¼ oz) modelling paste in half and colour light brown and mid-brown. Make Sooty's foot pads and Scampi's plaster. Thinly roll out the remaining sugarpaste and cut out a 30cm (12 inch) circle. Lift carefully and position over the cake, encouraging the pleats. Push up around Soo, Sweep and Scampi so it looks like they are peeping out from underneath.

6 Make a card template using the star outline on page 89. Thinly roll out the remaining black modelling paste and cut out a star using the template. Stick on the top of the cake using a little sugar glue. Position Sooty on top, then stick his wand in place.

Country Companions™

Cute Edward Hedgehog, Max Mole
and Ladybirds One, Two, Three are all
characters from Gordon Fraser's

Country Companions™

They all live together with their friends in a
village called Woodstump.

MATERIALS

1 litre (2 pint/5 cup) and 750ml
(1 ¼ pint/3 cup) bowl-shaped cakes
(page 84)
25cm (10 inch) square cake board
1.27kg (2lb 9oz) sugarpaste (rolled
fondant)
410g (13oz) buttercream
390g (12 ½ oz) modelling paste
red, blue, cream, brown, dark
brown, green, black and yellow
food colouring pastes
cool boiled water
sugar glue
black, cream and red dusting powders (petal dusts/blossom tints)
icing (confectioners') sugar

☆

EQUIPMENT

large and small rolling pins
sharp knife
plastic dowelling rod
large star and no. 4 plain piping
tubes (tips)
3.5cm (1 ½ inch) and 8.5cm
(3 ½ inch) circle cutters
stiff bristle medium paintbrush
fine paintbrush and flat-ended
dusting brush
cocktail sticks (toothpicks)
card for template
daisy cutter
foam sheet
small piece of cotton net

BOARD & CAKE

1 Thinly roll out 90g (3oz) sugarpaste
and cut a 3.5–5cm (1 ½–2 inch) strip
for the front of the cake board. Press in
position, making an uneven surface, and
trim away excess. Roll the trimmings into
small balls and stick some on
the strip to represent earth,
using a little sugar glue.
Make extra 'earth' and put
aside. To make the rug,
colour 250g (8oz) sug-
arpaste red and 170g (5 ½
oz) blue. Roll out the red.
Thinly roll out 60g (2oz) of
the blue and cut in strips.
Arrange the blue strips in a
checkered pattern over the
red sugarpaste, sticking
with a little sugar glue. Roll
the rolling pin over the surface to inlay. Cut the front
straight, stick the rug on the
cake board, leaving the
'earth' strip visible, and lift
the front edge for Max
Mole. Trim off excess paste
and reserve the red trim-
mings. Trim the crusts from

each cake, keeping the tops rounded
where each has risen. Slice the front of
the small cake a little flat for the face.

EDWARD HEDGEHOG

2 Split and fill the large cake with buttercream. Spread a thin layer of buttercream over each cake to help the
sugarpaste stick. Colour 750g (1½lb) sugarpaste pale cream. Roll out 410g (13oz)
and use to cover the large cake. Position
the small cake on top of the large cake
and push a dowelling rod down through
the top to help hold the head in place.
Roll two sausage shapes for the arms,

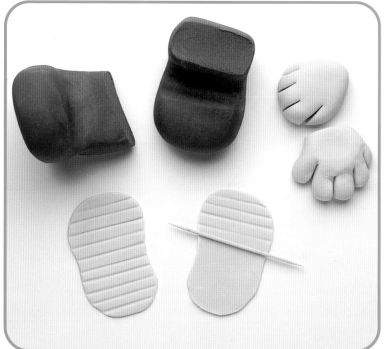

using 75g (2½oz) cream paste for each, and cut the ends straight. Stick in place using a little sugar glue. Pad out the face using 30g (1oz) paste for the muzzle and both cheeks. Press the tip of a large star piping tube into the sugarpaste repeatedly, all over the body and arms.

3 Roll out the remaining pale cream sugarpaste and cover Edward's face, smoothing around the back. Reserve the trimmings. Texture the top and sides of the head with the star tube, as before. Press the 3.5cm (1½ inch) circle cutter into the muzzle to mark Edward's smile and dimple the corners by pressing in the tip of a no. 4 plain piping tube at an angle. Using a knife, make cuts around the cheeks and muzzle, drawing the knife outwards to stretch the sugarpaste. Roll out the remaining blue sugarpaste and cut an 8.5cm (3½ inch) circle. Position over the back of Edward's head for his cap. Using the trimmings, model a small ball for the centre and cut out the peak, sticking in place with sugar glue. Texture a small piece of the cream sugarpaste trimmings and stick on the back of the cap for the opening. Dilute some brown and dark brown food colouring pastes separately with cool boiled water. Stipple the colours over the hedgehog, using the stiff paintbrush (see page 13), leaving his tummy unpainted. Stipple the textured

patch on the cap. Paint the front piece of the cake board and the earth. Dilute the dark brown a little more and paint a thin coat around Edward's eye area and around his cheeks. Stipple the same colour around the edge of his tummy, fading out to the centre. Leave to dry, then position the cake on the cake board.

4 Colour 125g (4oz) modelling paste pale cream. Using 60g (2oz), make Edward Hedgehog's two hands and the soles of his wellies, using a card template (see page 89) and indenting with a cocktail stick. Colour 220g (7oz) modelling paste green. Split in half and shape the pieces into two wellies, cutting the top of each straight. Reserve the green trimmings. Stick the wellies in place and add the soles. Using the diluted dark brown, paint a thin coat over the soles. Stick the hands in place.

MAX MOLE

5 Using the remaining pale cream modelling paste, shape a head for Max Mole with a pointed muzzle. Roll a ball for his nose and shape a hand. Using the black, cream and red dusting powders and the flat-ended dusting brush, dust colour over Max Mole, building up the colour little by little. Make the black quite dense around the back of his head and fade it out around his face. Indent his smile by pressing in the end of the

24

DAISIES & LADYBIRDS

6 Make the daisies using 22g (¾oz) modelling paste. To make the first daisy, thinly roll out some paste and cut out two daisy shapes using the daisy cutter. Place on a foam sheet. Indent the centre of each using the end of a paintbrush, and mark the centre of each petal with a cocktail stick. Stick one on top of the other. Make two more daisies. Colour 7g (¼oz) modelling paste yellow. Model three small balls and press on to a piece of cotton net to indent a pattern. Stick in place with a little sugar glue. With the green trimmings, make the daisy stems and stick under Edward Hedgehog's hand. To make grass, roll out more green trimmings and press the tip of the star nozzle repeatedly into the paste. Stick small pieces on the board and on Max Mole's head. Using the red sugarpaste and black modelling paste trimmings, make the ladybirds, One, Two, Three. Shape small fat ovals of red paste and indent down the centre of each with a cocktail stick. Add tiny black spots and heads.

no. 4 piping tube at an angle, and dimple using the tip. Dust some cream over Max Mole's face and hand, and over Edward Hedgehog's hands. Weaken the red by adding a little loose icing sugar, then dust over the cheeks of both characters, building up the colour gradually. Dust a little red on Max Mole's nose. Stick Max Mole's head and hand in position with a little sugar glue and stick some earth on top of his head. Colour 15g (½oz) modelling paste black and make Edward Hedgehog's nose, eyes and eyebrows, and Max Mole's eyes. Stick a minute piece of white on to each eye to highlight. Reserve the black trimmings.

PEANUTS™

Snoopy and Woodstock belong to the famous PEANUTS™ group of characters. Here, Snoopy is in his favourite position, snoozing on his kennel.

MATERIALS

25cm (10 inch) square cake
25cm (10 inch) oval cake board
410g (13oz) buttercream
1.05kg (2lb 1½oz) sugarpaste
(rolled fondant)
125g (4oz) modelling paste
black, red, yellow and green food
colouring pastes
clear alcohol (gin or vodka) or cool
boiled water
sugar glue

☆

EQUIPMENT

sharp knife
ruler
large rolling pin
medium paintbrush
card for template
star piping tube (tip)

Tip

To avoid undue mess and to regulate amounts, apply food colouring to all icing and modelling pastes using cocktail sticks (toothpicks).

KENNEL

1 Trim the crust from the cake. To make the kennel roof, cut a 15cm (6 inch) strip from the cake and cut in half. Sandwich one piece on top of the other with buttercream and trim to make the roof shape. Cut the remaining cake in half and sandwich together with buttercream to make the kennel base. Sandwich the roof on top. Position the cake on the cake board. Spread a thin layer of buttercream over the surface of the cake to help the sugarpaste stick.

2 Roll out 315g (10oz) sugarpaste and cut out pieces to fit the kennel base, covering the ends first, then the sides. Smooth the joins closed at each corner. Mark the lines on each end of the kennel using a knife. Cut

an arched doorway out of the sugarpaste on the front end. Thinly roll out the sugarpaste trimmings and, using the piece cut out from the doorway as a template, cut out a piece to fill the doorway. Mark lines on the sides of the kennel with a knife. Dilute a little black food colouring paste with clear alcohol and paint the doorway. Roll out 75g (2½oz) sugarpaste and cut strips to fill the gap and cover the underside of the kennel roof. Roll out 410g (13oz) sugarpaste and cut pieces to fit the front and back triangles of the kennel roof, then roll out and cut a piece to cover the top, smoothing the joins closed as before. Mark the lines on the roof. Dilute red food colouring with clear alcohol and paint the kennel roof. Put aside to dry.

SNOOPY

3 Model a fat teardrop shape for Snoopy's body using 30g (1oz) modelling paste. Trim off the point. Using 15g (½ oz) paste, model his arms and legs, marking his fingers and toes with a knife. With 45g (1½ oz) paste, model Snoopy's head, shaping a rounded muzzle. Colour a little modelling paste red and make Snoopy's collar. Make a card template for Snoopy's ears using the outline on page 89. Colour 7g (¼ oz) modelling paste black and make Snoopy's ears (using the template as a guide), nose and eyes, and two tiny eyes for Woodstock.

WOODSTOCK

4 Colour the remaining modelling paste yellow and split in half. Model Woodstock's head using one piece, cut a slit down the back of his head and open slightly. Make four cuts in the paste on each side of the slit and fan out and

shape the feathers. With the remaining yellow paste, make his body, feet, wings and tail, marking the lines with a knife.

TO FINISH

5 Assemble Snoopy and Woodstock on the top of the kennel roof using sugar glue to secure. Colour the remaining sugarpaste green. Roll out pieces and cover the board up to and around the base of the kennel. For the grass effect, press the tip of a star piping tube into the sugarpaste repeatedly, teasing up the sugarpaste a little higher around the base of the kennel.

Tip Always knead the paste until warm and pliable before use. Use icing (confectioners') sugar when rolling out and keep moving the paste around to prevent sticking.

The Wind in the Willows

Generations of children have enjoyed reading the riverbank adventures of Toad, Ratty and Mole in Kenneth Grahame's *The Wind in the Willows.*

WHEELS

1 Make the caravan wheels first to allow plenty of drying time. Divide 45g (1½oz) modelling paste in two, roll out one half and cut out four 5cm (2 inch) circles. Indent a small circle in the centre of each, then cut out the spokes with a sharp knife. Roll out the remaining paste and cut out the wheels using 5cm (2 inch) and 6.5cm (2½inch) circle cutters. Dilute a little brown food colouring paste with alcohol and paint the spokes. Do the same with the wheels, using red. Colour the paste trimmings green and red, and make the wheel bolts. Colour the royal icing red. Using a no. 2 plain piping tube, pipe a little royal icing on the ends of the spokes and position the wheels over the top, then stick the wheel bolts in place. Put the wheels aside to dry. Reserve the remaining royal icing.

CAKE BOARD & CARAVAN

2 Roll out 315g (10oz) sugarpaste and use to cover the cake board. Put aside to dry. Trim the top from the cake where it has risen, and trim off the crust. Cut the cake as shown in the diagram.

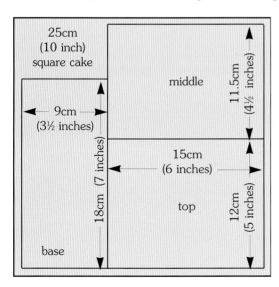

25cm (10 inch) square cake

middle

9cm (3½ inches)

11.5cm (4½ inches)

15cm (6 inches)

18cm (7 inches)

top

12cm (5 inches)

base

MATERIALS

25cm (10 inch) square cake
25cm (10 inch) petal-shaped cake board
170g (5½oz) modelling paste
30g (1oz) royal icing
1.1kg (2lb 3oz) sugarpaste (rolled fondant)
500g (1lb) buttercream
brown, red, green, black, yellow, lilac, blue, pink and dark green food colouring pastes
clear alcohol (gin or vodka) or cool boiled water
sugar glue

☆

EQUIPMENT

large and small rolling pins
5cm (2 inch), 1cm (½inch), 6.5cm (2½ inch) circle cutters
sharp knife
medium and fine paintbrushes
greaseproof paper piping bag
no. 2 plain piping tube (tip)
ruler
cocktail sticks (toothpicks)
small square cutter
card for template
pieces of foam

THE WIND IN THE WILLOWS
cake created by kind permission of
The University Chest, Oxford.

effect step for the front. Thinly roll out the trimmings and cut the wood effect strips for around the caravan, sticking in place with a little sugar glue.

DOORS & WINDOWS

5 Using 22g (¾ oz) of the remaining pale yellow sugarpaste, roll out and cut a curved piece to cover the cake above the door and windows at the front of the caravan. Mark wooden slats with a knife and scratch on the woodgrain effect as before. Cut out three diamonds above the door. Colour some paste trimmings black, roll out and cut out three diamonds to fill the spaces. Very thinly roll out 15g (½ oz) and cut a length to cover the cake behind the window and top half of the door. Using 30g (1oz), roll out and cut strips for the door frame and stick in place, then measure the remaining space and cut out the windows and door, using a small square cutter to cut the window panes. Mark the wood effect as before. Paint the door red. Dilute a little brown food colouring paste with alcohol and paint the windows, step, wood effect trim around the caravan, and the door frame. Colour 45g (1 ½ oz) modelling paste pale green. Put aside 7g (¼ oz), then make four shutters, cutting a small diamond in the centre of each. Mark a woodgrain effect as before. Model two green doorknobs and stick one each on the top and bottom parts of the door.

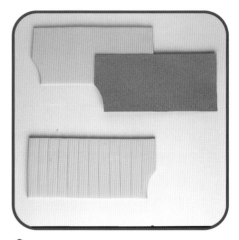

6 Using the remaining pale yellow sugarpaste, cut a piece to fit the remaining uncovered part at the back of the caravan. Make a card template for the side pieces (see page 92) and cut out two, indenting the lines and marking with a woodgrain effect as before. Carefully position on the cake, then trim out a window in the centre of each side. Very thinly roll out the trimmings and use to fill the two side windows. Well dilute a little black food colouring paste and paint a wash over the inside of the front door and all the window areas. Stick the windows and shutters in place. Make the two small side window bars and paint brown as before. Colour the remaining sugarpaste pale lilac, roll out and use to cover the caravan roof. Indent the zig-zag pattern at the front and back using a knife. Indent a circle in the side of the roof using the end of a piping tube and mark nail holes just inside the circle with

3 Arrange the cake layers one on top of the other, with the base protruding at the front. Trim out the front step at the base. Trim the curved roof and trim down the sides to neaten. Sandwich the layers together using buttercream, then spread a thin layer of buttercream over the cake to help the sugarpaste stick.

4 Measure around the base of the cake, then thinly roll out 60g (2oz) sugarpaste and cut a length no more than 2.5cm (1 inch) in width that will fit around the base of the cake. Stick in position. Dilute a little black food colouring paste with alcohol and paint the strip black. Colour 500g (1lb) sugarpaste pale yellow. Roll out 30g (1oz), then measure and cut two strips to fit the step risers at the front of the caravan, marking the woodgrain effect with a cocktail stick (see page 12). Roll out 75g (2 ½oz) yellow paste, and cut two curved side pieces to cover the bottom layer of cake only, marking the woodgrain effect as before. Roll out the trimmings and cut out a piece for the bottom layer at the back of the caravan. Using 60g (2oz) pale yellow sugarpaste, roll out and cut the wood

a cocktail stick. With the pale yellow trimmings, model a chimney pot and stick it in place with a little sugar glue. Using the remaining red royal icing, stick the wheels in position and the two door pieces in place. If necessary, use pieces of foam for support whilst drying.

RATTY

7 First colour 7g (¼ oz) modelling paste blue, 7g (¼ oz) red, 15g (½ oz) brown, 7g (¼ oz) black and a tiny amount pink. Using three-quarters of the blue, model Ratty's trousers first, bending in the middle for the knees, and stick in place on the caravan step. Using half the red paste, make Ratty's top, indenting down the front with a knife. Model his shoes using the remaining red paste. As each piece is made, stick it in place using a little sugar glue. With the remaining pale green, cut out Ratty's jacket and model two sleeves. Using a little of the brown, model two hands, then make Ratty's head, indenting his mouth with a knife and then pushing in the end of a paintbrush to open it. Use a cocktail stick to

scratch a few fur lines over the surface. Model four blue buttons with a tiny amount of the remaining blue paste and, with the pink, model two ears and a nose, reserving a minute amount to make Mole's nose. Make Ratty's two tiny eyes using black, then stick a minute white dot on each eye to give a sparkle.

TOAD

8 Colour 15g (½ oz) modelling paste dark green, a little yellow and 7g (¼ oz) green. Split the dark green modelling paste in half and make Toad's trousers with one piece and his jacket and sleeves with the other. Stick each piece in position on the step as it is made. Model Toad's top using yellow modelling paste, and make his neck tie with the remaining blue. Using a little of the remaining brown, model his shoes. With the green modelling paste, make Toad's hands, head and eyes, making his mouth as before but much wider and pushing up the top lip. Finish his eyes with minute amounts of white and black modelling paste.

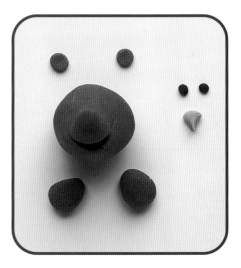

MOLE

9 Use the remaining brown modelling paste to make Mole's face with a pointed muzzle, cutting open his mouth and pushing down his bottom lip. Make two tiny ears and his hands. Stick in place at the open door and add a tiny pink nose and two tiny black eyes. Paint Mole's head with diluted black food colouring.

TO FINISH

10 With the remaining red and black modelling paste, make tiny poppies for around the base of the caravan. Dilute some green, dark green, yellow, red and black food colouring paste with alcohol. Stipple different greens over the cake board using a mixture of the greens and the yellow, keeping the brush quite dry (see page 13). Leave the stippled effect to dry thoroughly before painting some leaves on the board. Paint some poppies on the board, using the diluted red and black colouring.

Tip

Thoroughly remove excess icing (confectioners') sugar from the surface of dried paste before attempting any painting or drawing, as the colours might spread.

Postman Pat™

Postman Pat and his black and white cat, Jess, have arrived on the party table to deliver a tasty treat for any birthday girl or boy.

BOARD & CAKE

1 Colour 410g (13oz) sugarpaste grey (using a little black colouring). Roll out and use to cover the cake board. Press the rolling pin into the sugarpaste to indent lines across the board. Model flattened balls for the pebbles, using the trimmings, and stick in place. Put the board aside to dry. Trim the crust from the cake, then cut it exactly in half. Trim 5cm (2 inches) from the length of one half, cutting down at an outward angle to shape the windscreen. Position on top of the other cake half. Cut a slice from the remaining piece and place on the bonnet. Trim around the base of the van, cutting in at an angle, and trim the bonnet to round off. Sandwich the layers of cake together using buttercream, then spread a thin layer of buttercream over the whole surface of the cake to help the sugarpaste stick.

VAN

2 Colour 100g (3 ½ oz) sugarpaste black. Roll out thinly and cut a 1cm (½ inch) wide strip at least 50cm (21 inches) in length. Roll up, position against the base of the van and carefully unroll around the base, smoothing the join closed. Thinly roll out the trimmings and cut out two 4cm (1 ½ inch) circles. Cut each circle in half and stick on the side of the van to cover where the wheels will go. Roll out the remaining white sugarpaste and use to cover the van, trimming the base in line with the black. Mark the windscreen, windows, bonnet, doors and lines around the van using the back of a knife. Dilute a little red food colouring with cool boiled water and paint the van red, leaving a strip at the front of the bonnet, and the windscreen and side and back windows unpainted. Lift the cake carefully, supporting it underneath and taking care not to mark the soft sugarpaste, and position on the cake board.

MATERIALS

18cm (7 inch) square cake
30cm (12 inch) oval cake board
1.25kg (2½lb) sugarpaste (rolled fondant)
315g (10oz) buttercream
315g (10oz) modelling paste
30g (1oz) royal icing
black, red, green, pink, yellow, blue, flesh, orange and golden brown food colouring pastes
cool boiled water
sugar glue
black food colouring pen

☆

EQUIPMENT

large and small rolling pins
sharp knife
fine paintbrush
2cm (¾ inch) and 4cm (1½ inch) circle cutters
no. 1 plain piping tube (tip)
greaseproof paper
cocktail stick (toothpick)
greaseproof paper piping bags

Tip

When a large piece of sugarpaste (rolled fondant) is rolled out, lift by folding over the rolling pin. This will make it easier to position.

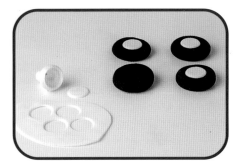

JESS

4 Using the photograph, right, as a guide, model Jess the cat using 15g (½ oz) black modelling paste. Assemble Jess in his pose, then stick on pieces of white modelling paste for his eyes, muzzle, ears, chest, tummy, tail and two front paws, marking the fur lines with a knife. Colour a minute piece of modelling paste pale green and another pink. Make Jess's pink nose and green eyes with tiny black pupils. When dry, draw in his smile using a black food colouring pen. Position Jess on the bonnet of the van. With 7g (¼ oz) black modelling paste, make the windscreen wiper, steering wheel and two side mirrors. Colour 7g (¼ oz) modelling paste yellow. Roll out thinly and cut out two licence plates. Stick tiny flattened balls of yellow on to the indicator lights.

POSTMAN PAT

5 First colour 60g (2oz) modelling paste blue, 15g (½ oz) flesh-coloured and 7g (¼ oz) orange. Set aside a minute amount of black modelling paste for Pat's tie and cap visor, then use the remainder to make his shoes, indenting around the base for his soles. Make his trousers next, using 22g (¾ oz) blue

3 To make the wheels, colour 60g (2oz) modelling paste black. Divide half into four equally sized pieces and model four flattened ball shapes. Thinly roll out 7g (¼ oz) white modelling paste and cut out four inner wheels using a 2cm (¾ inch) circle cutter. Stick the wheels in place using a little sugar glue. Thinly roll out 45g (1½ oz) white modelling paste, and cut out the front grille, indenting with a knife. Cut strips for the bumpers, and cut out headlights using the 2cm (¾ inch) circle cutter. Indent the centre of each headlight with the large end of a no. 1 plain piping tube. Model the door handles, and indicator lights for the back and front. Dilute a little black food colouring paste with cool boiled water to make a very pale grey. Keeping the brush quite dry, paint a little over all the white parts of the van to give a shiny effect.

paste, and stick on to his shoes using a little sugar glue. To make Pat's jacket, model a flattened ball using 30g (1oz) blue paste, and cut either side for his sleeves. Gently twist the sleeves down, bend halfway along for the elbows, then hollow out the ends using the end of a paintbrush. Indent down the centre of the jacket using a knife, then press the knife-point down on to the chest to indent. Stick the jacket on top of the trousers, and stick in position against the van. Using 15g (½ oz) white modelling paste, make Pat's shirt and collar, stick in place, then cut out all the letters in the postbag, and put aside to dry. Using the flesh modelling paste, make Pat's head, ears, nose and hands, and stick in place. With the remaining blue, make Pat's cap, coat collar and lapels, and stick in place. Roll tiny balls of orange modelling paste and stick over Pat's head for his hair. Make his tie and cap visor from the remaining black paste.

TO FINISH

6 Colour the remaining modelling paste golden brown and model the open postbag and parcels. Colour the royal icing yellow. Trace the Royal Mail lettering (page 90) on to greaseproof paper. Using a cocktail stick, scribe the outline on to both sides of the van. Using the no. 1 piping tube, pipe the string on the parcels, the emblem on Postman Pat's cap, and the Royal Mail signs. Using a black food colouring pen, address the letters, draw the stamps, and draw features on Postman Pat's face. Write 'PAT 1' on the licence plates. Paint a little diluted red on to each stamp.

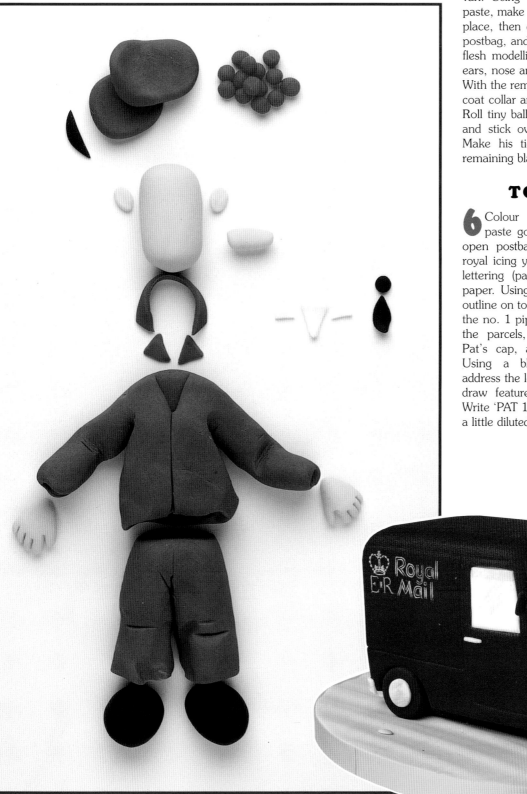

MATERIALS

two 1 litre (2 pint/5 cup) bowl
cakes (page 84)
30cm (12 inch) oval petal-shaped
cake board
1.6kg (3lb 2oz) sugarpaste (rolled
fondant)
345g (11oz) buttercream
60g (2oz) pastillage
green, flesh, blue, pink, brown,
black, yellow and golden brown
food colouring pastes
sugar glue
black food colouring pen

EQUIPMENT

sharp knife
large and small rolling pins
fine paintbrush
card for templates
scissors
piece of foam
no. 4 plain piping tube (tip)

Tip

Wear plastic gloves when
kneading the colours into
paste as the food colouring
might stain your hands.

**The cheekiest, nippiest little helicopter ever,
Budgie is flying his way to popularity. His free-
spinning rotor-blade will make sure any child's
birthday party takes off.**

BOARD & CAKES

1 Colour 410g (13oz) sugarpaste green, roll out and use to cover the cake board. Put aside to dry. Trim the crust from the cakes and put together to make a ball. Trim one side to flatten slightly for Budgie's face. Sandwich the two cakes together with buttercream, then spread a thin layer of buttercream over the surface of the cake to help the sugarpaste stick.

BUDGIE'S FACE

2 Colour 250g (8oz) sugarpaste flesh-coloured. Using 60g (2oz), model a ball and press it on to the centre of Budgie's face to pad out his nose, smoothing either side in line with the sur-

face of the cake. To pad out his cheeks and chin, split 22g (¾ oz) flesh-coloured paste into three equally sized pieces. Roll two balls and press on to the cake on either side of Budgie's nose. For his chin, roll a sausage shape, thin it at either end, curve up the ends and press into position, smoothing the ends in line with the surface of the cake.

3 Roll out the remaining flesh-coloured paste and use to cover Budgie's face, sticking with sugar glue where necessary. Smooth the paste around the padding and trim across the top of his nose and upwards around his eye area. Trim excess paste from around his cheeks down to his chin. Colour 45g (1 ½ oz) sugarpaste pale blue. Make card templates for the eye area and mouth, using the outlines on page 92. Roll out

38

foam until dry. Using the remaining blue, cut out a pouch for teddy and stick on the side of Budgie, marking a square 'door' at the top as before. Reserve the trimmings. Colour 315g (10oz) sugarpaste yellow. Roll out 155g (5oz), and cut out a circle to fit on top of Budgie for his cap. Before making the visor, colour 22g (¾oz) sugarpaste dark golden brown and make pointed teardrop pieces for Budgie's hair and six tiny freckles. Stick the hair pieces on top of his eye area, making the hair fuller in the centre. Stick the freckles on Budgie's cheeks. Make a card template for the cap visor, using the outline on page 92. Roll out 45g (1½oz) yellow sugarpaste and cut out the visor. Stick in place along the front of the cap, curving up and over Budgie's hair.

ROTOR-BLADES

5 Make a 'B' template (see page 92). Thinly roll out the remaining blue sugarpaste, cut out the initial, and stick on top of Budgie's cap. Model a flattened ball with the blue trimmings and put aside. Colour the pastillage pale grey. Using 7g (¼oz), first roll two very thin pieces of pastillage for the rotor supports and put aside, then model the tail rotor and cut a small circle in the centre, using the tip of a no. 4 plain piping tube. Check the rotor support fits into the hole. Using 30g (1oz) grey pastillage, roll a sausage and, using the photograph below as a guide, roll both ends with a

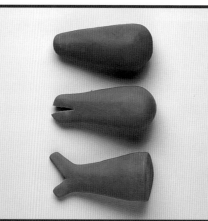

the blue paste and cut out the eye area using the template. Stick in place, then indent a line down the centre with the back of a knife. Colour 7g (¼oz) sugarpaste dark pink/brown. Roll out thinly and cut out Budgie's smile using the template. Reserve the trimmings. Using 15g (½oz) white sugarpaste, model Budgie's eyes and cut a strip for his teeth. With some of the trimmings, model a minute white highlight for each eye. Knead the remaining white trimmings into the pink/brown trimmings to obtain a paler pink/brown paste, and model Budgie's tongue. Colour 7g (¼oz) sugarpaste dark grey (using a little black colouring) and model the tip of his nose, sticking in place with sugar glue. Colour 7g (¼oz) sugarpaste black. Reserve a minute amount for the teddy's nose, then make Budgie's eyes and eyebrows. Stick all of Budgie's features in place and position the cake on the cake board.

TAIL, CAP & HAIR

4 Colour 470g (15oz) sugarpaste blue. Roll out 315g (10oz) and use to cover around the back of Budgie, leaving the top of his head uncovered for his cap. Indent lines for the door and cut out the door window. Using 100g (3½oz) blue paste, model his tail using the photograph, above, as a guide. Stick in position with a little sugar glue, smoothing the join closed. Support with a piece of

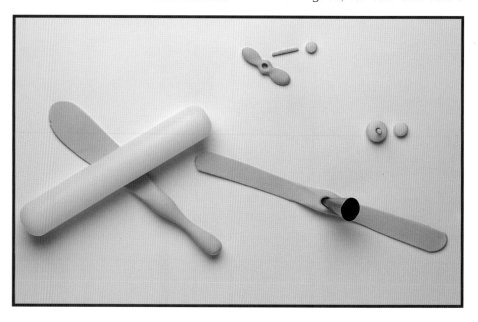

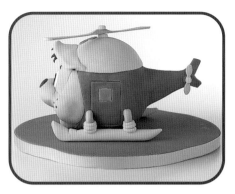

Split 75g (2 ½ oz) yellow sugarpaste in two and model the socks for the skids, turning up and indenting at the front with a knife. With the remaining yellow, make the tail stabilizer and stick in place, then model twelve flattened balls for the sock-tops and stick together in threes. Assemble the skid socks on the cake board with the grey skid supports resting against the sides of Budgie. Make the teddy using the remaining sugarpaste, indenting the centre of each ear with the end of a paintbrush. Make his nose from the tiny piece of reserved black sugarpaste. When the cake is dry, draw the eyes on teddy using a black food colouring pen.

small rolling pin until the piece has a total length of about 20cm (8 inches), leaving the centre thick. Trim excess paste from either side. Cut a small circle in the centre as before, then put aside to dry. Using 7g (¼ oz) yellow sugarpaste, roll one large, one medium and one small ball, and slightly flatten each. Push a rotor support in the centre of the large ball, sticking with sugar glue. When the large rotor is completely dry, position over the rotor support and stick the medium ball on top. Do the same for the tail rotor, sticking the rotor support into the blue flattened ball made earlier. Stick both rotors in position on the cake.

TO FINISH

6 Using 7g (¼ oz) grey pastillage, cut out a square to fill the door window. Roll a sausage with the remaining grey pastillage and cut into four. Bend each halfway along to make the skid supports.

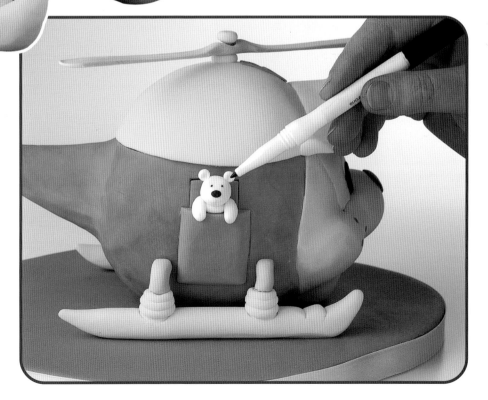

41

FOREVER·FRIENDS ™

Cute and cuddly, the Forever Friends bears are as popular with adults as with children.

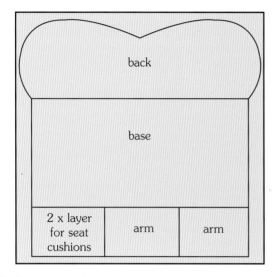

back
base

| 2 x layer for seat cushions | arm | arm |

BOARD, SOFA & CUSHIONS

1 Roll out 500g (1lb) sugarpaste and use to cover the cake board. Put aside to dry. Trim the crust from the cake and cut into pieces as shown in the diagram (above).

2 Assemble the cake pieces to make the sofa, trimming to shape the back and arms. Using buttercream, sandwich the pieces together, then spread a thin layer of buttercream over the surface of the cake to help the sugarpaste stick. Roll out the remaining sugarpaste and cover the sofa, covering the front first and smoothing around the seat and arms. Trim the pleats from the corners at the back and smooth the joins closed. Using a knife, mark the line for the seat cushion. Place the cake on the board.

3 Using the sugarpaste trimmings, model two cushions. Using 22g (¾ oz) modelling paste, roll very thin sausage shapes. Using a cocktail stick, make angled indentations along the sausage shapes, creating a rope effect. Stick around the edges of each cushion and make tassels for each corner. Make the same rope effect trim for the sofa, sticking in place with a little sugar

MATERIALS

25cm (10 inch) square cake
36cm (14 inch) oval cake board
1.5kg (3lb) sugarpaste (rolled fondant)
440g (14oz) buttercream
500g (1lb) modelling paste
pink, green, golden brown and black food colouring pastes
sugar glue
cool boiled water
pink dusting powder (petal dust/blossom tint)
45g (1½oz) royal icing

☆

EQUIPMENT

sharp knife
large and small rolling pins
cocktail sticks (toothpicks)
medium and fine paintbrushes
small circle cutter
greaseproof paper piping bag

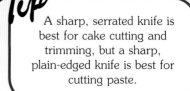

Tip
A sharp, serrated knife is best for cake cutting and trimming, but a sharp, plain-edged knife is best for cutting paste.

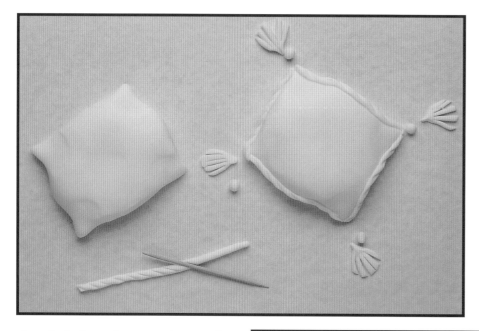

glue. Stick the cushions in place on the sofa. Dilute some pink food colouring paste with cool boiled water to make a pale, well-diluted pink. Dilute some more, making a stronger pink. To paint the checkered design on the sofa, use a medium paintbrush and the stronger pink (see page 11). Paint horizontal lines, leave to dry, then paint vertical lines. Stipple the design over each cushion (see page 13). Using the well-diluted pink, paint a thin coat over the cake board, keeping the brush quite dry to obtain a lined effect. Edge with stronger pink. Dilute a little green food colouring paste and paint the rose stalks and leaves on the board. Use the strong pink to paint the roses, the patterns on the cushions (see page 91) and the rope-effect edging.

BEARS

4 To make the Forever Friends bears, first colour 440g (14oz) modelling paste golden brown. Model each body using 90g (3oz) paste, and stick them in place on the sofa with a little sugar glue. Model the heads, using 75g (2½oz) paste for each. Mark down the centre of each one with a knife. With the remaining paste, make legs, arms and ears. Colour 7g (¼oz) modelling paste a paler golden brown and make two muzzles. Indent down the centre of each with a knife and mark on the bears' smiles with a small circle cutter pushed in at an upward angle. Dimple each corner by pressing in the tip of a cocktail stick. Colour a

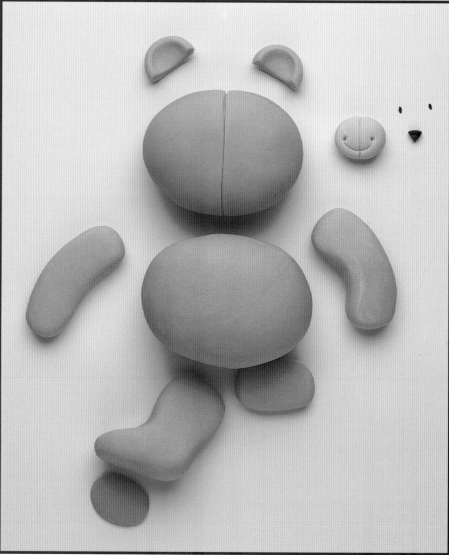

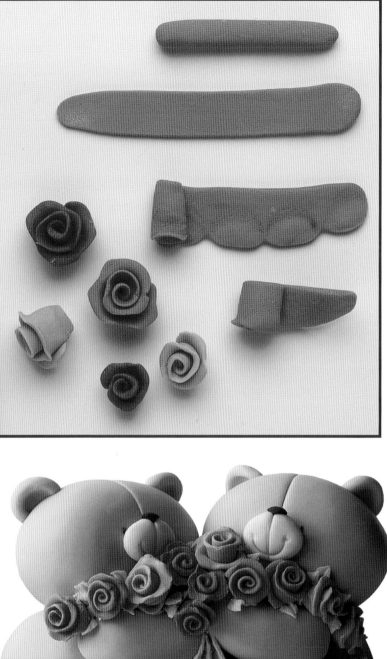

minute amount of modelling paste black and make the bears' noses and eyes. Dust a little pink dusting powder on their ears and over their cheeks to give a blush. Colour the remaining modelling paste different shades of pink. Make two foot pads for the bears with a little pale pink paste and stick in place.

ROSES

5 To make a rose, roll a sausage of pink paste, then roll flat. Scallop one edge by pressing along the edge of the paste with your fingertip, turn over,

moisten, then carefully roll up. Using a damp paintbrush, open the petals. Make 12–14 roses in various shades of pink, and put aside to dry.

6 Colour the royal icing green. Using a piping bag with a small 'V' cut in the tip, stick the roses in the bears' arms, and pipe the stalks and leaves.

MATERIALS

20cm (8 inch) round cake
30cm (12 inch) round cake board
1kg (2lb) sugarpaste (rolled fondant)
375g (12oz) buttercream
95g (3 ¼ oz) modelling paste
60g (2oz) royal icing
brown, blue, black, flesh, yellow,
red and green food colouring
pastes
clear alcohol (gin or vodka) or cool
boiled water
sugar glue
raw dried spaghetti
black food colouring pen

☆

EQUIPMENT

sharp knife
large rolling pin
card for templates
ruler
cocktail sticks (toothpicks)
fine and medium paintbrushes
greaseproof paper piping bag

Tip
You may wish to remove
the piece of sugarpaste (rolled
fondant) from the area of
cake board on which the cake
will sit. Because the cake is
moist, the sugarpaste underneath has a tendency to
become slightly sticky.

World-famous Popeye the Sailorman eats his spinach to get big and strong. Perhaps the kids will now eat their greens – after the cake is all gone, of course!

CAKE & BOARD

1 Roll out 375g (12oz) sugarpaste and use to cover the cake board. Put aside to dry. Trim the crust from the cake and slice the top flat. Cut a layer in the cake, then sandwich back together with buttercream. Spread a thin layer of but-tercream over the surface of the cake to help the sugarpaste stick. Position the cake on the cake board. Roll out the remaining sugarpaste and use to cover the cake completely, trimming around the base.

BOAT

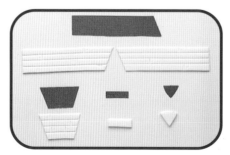

2 Make card templates for the boat pieces (see page 89). Roll out 30g (1oz) modelling paste and cut out two sides, a back and a front using the card templates. Make a wood effect by indenting the pieces with a ruler. Mark each joint and nail hole with a knife and cocktail stick. Cut the pieces for inside the boat using the trimmings. Stick the boat together with sugar glue and leave to firm up a little.

3 Position the boat on the top of the cake. Dilute a little brown food colouring paste with clear alcohol. With the medium paintbrush, paint a colour-wash over the boat to give a streaky, wood-like effect (see page 12). Using royal icing and a piping bag with a hole cut in the tip, pipe a line around the base of the cake, then smooth the royal icing in line with the surface of the cake using your finger. When the painted boat

elling paste flesh-coloured, and make Popeye's head, chin, nose, ears, arms and hands in one piece, tiny ball elbows and neck. Push a short length of raw spaghetti into the neck, leaving enough exposed at each end to support the figure when assembled. Stick Popeye's chin and nose in place, then push the end of a paintbrush in to make his open mouth. Stick his pipe in place. Split 7g (¼ oz) modelling paste in half. Make Popeye's hat with one piece, then colour the other piece yellow. Using a minute amount of yellow, model and position three buttons. (Reserve the remaining yellow.) Assemble Popeye in the boat using sugar glue to secure. Split another 7g (¼ oz) paste in two. Put one piece aside for the oars, then colour the other piece red. Roll out the red, and cut out Popeye's collar, sticking in place with sugar glue.

is dry, pipe royal icing around the base of the boat, flicking it up a little to make 'waves'.

POPEYE

4 Colour 7g (¼ oz) modelling paste blue. Roll two ball shapes for Popeye's legs, two tiny balls for his knees and two flattened ball shapes for his rolled-up sleeves. Colour 7g (¼ oz) modelling paste brown. Model Popeye's shoes, indenting the front of each with a knife to mark the soles. Colour 15g (½ oz) black. Make Popeye's top, short sleeves and pipe. Colour 15g (½ oz) mod-

OARS & SPINACH

5 Cut two 7.5cm (3 inch) lengths of raw spaghetti. Make two oars using the reserved piece of modelling paste, sticking the paste to the end of each length of spaghetti with sugar glue. Paint the oars with a brown wash, as for the boat. Carefully push the ends of the oars into Popeye's hands, sticking in place resting against the sides of the boat. Colour the remaining modelling paste grey (using a little black colouring) and make two spinach cans. Cut two strips from the remaining yellow paste and stick one around the centre of each can. Colour some trimmings green and make the spinach leaves. Place the spinach cans in the boat.

TO FINISH

6 Dilute a little blue food colouring paste with clear alcohol. Keeping the brush quite dry, paint the water effect on the cake and board. When the cake is completely dry, draw in Popeye's face, tattoos, collar stripe and all the 'ripple' lines on the cake using a black food colouring pen.

Thomas the Tank Engine

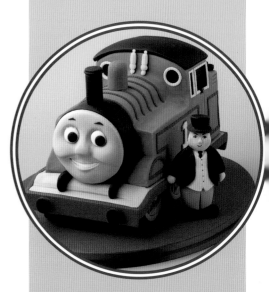

In the Rev. W. Awdry's famous stories, cheeky Thomas is always trying to please The Fat Controller, or Sir Topham Hatt as he is also known. As a colourful cake, he's bound to please everybody!

MATERIALS

30x20cm (12x8 inch) oblong cake (page 85)
30cm (12 inch) oval cake board
1.5kg (3lb) sugarpaste (rolled fondant)
440g (14oz) buttercream
470g (15oz) modelling paste
red, black, blue, yellow and flesh food colouring pastes
sugar glue
black food colouring pen
red dusting powder (petal dust/blossom tint)

☆

EQUIPMENT

large and small rolling pins
sharp knife
ruler
fine paintbrush
1cm (½ inch), 2cm (¾ inch), 2.5cm (1 inch), 4.5cm (1¾ inch), 5cm (2 inch) and 7.5cm (3 inch) circle cutters
card for templates
scissors

Tip If your cake has to be cut into shapes, store it in an airtight container for at least 6 hours before use to allow the texture to settle.

BOARD & CAKE

1 Colour 375g (12oz) sugarpaste red. Roll out and use to cover the cake board, then put aside to dry. Trim the crust from the cake and slice the top flat. Cut the cake into three equal pieces, each measuring just under 20x10cm (8x4 inches). Put two layers together, one on top of the other. To shape the top of the engine from the remaining sponge layer, trim a 2.5cm (1 inch) piece out of one end for the coal bunker, cutting down to two-thirds of the depth. Use the cut-out piece for the front chassis, shaping it by trimming the top into a curve. Measure 5cm (2 inches) from the coal bunker along the piece of cake, and cut the layer across into two pieces. Shape the 5cm (2 inch) section to become the cab by trimming either side to give it a sloping roof. Put the coal bunker and cab piece on top of the cake. Slice 4cm (1½ inches) from the width of the other half of the layer, and shape to make the rounded top of the engine. Position on top of the cake. Trim the middle layer of sponge either side of the engine to shape the side tanks and wheel covers, cutting in to round off the face.

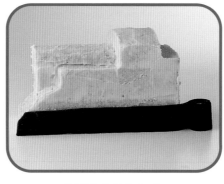

THOMAS

2 Use buttercream to sandwich the layers and stick all the cake pieces together. Stick the front chassis in place using buttercream, then spread a thin layer of buttercream over the surface of the cake to help the sugarpaste stick. Colour 125g (4oz) sugarpaste black. Thinly roll out half and cut a 2.5cm (1 inch) strip measuring at least 50cm

(20 inches) in length. Roll up, position the end on the side of Thomas and unroll around the base of the cake, leaving the front uncovered. Thinly roll out the trimmings and cut a strip for the front under the chassis.

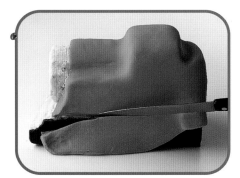

3 Colour 750g (1½lb) sugarpaste blue. Thickly roll out and use to cover Thomas. Cut away at the top at the front then down and around the side tanks and wheel covers. Trim away excess just above the black strip. (Reserve the blue trimmings.) Smooth the sugarpaste around Thomas's shape and pinch gently to encourage sharp edges. Mark three indented lines on either side of the coal bunker using the back of a knife. Position the cake on the cake board. Trim out the cab opening and small window on each side, and cut out the 'portholes' using a 2cm (¾inch) circle cutter. Indent lines for the cab doors on either side using the back of a knife. Model Thomas's dome from some of the blue trimmings and put

aside. Colour 250g (8oz) sugarpaste grey (using a little black colouring). Put aside 45g (1½oz), then roll out and cut a piece to cover the top of the front chassis. Cut various lengths 1cm (½inch) wide to fit either side and around the back of the engine, covering the join between the blue and black paste, and sticking in place with a little sugar glue. Colour 90g (3oz) modelling paste red, and roll out. Cut strips and stick in position at the front of the chassis, and along both sides and at the back of the engine. Reserve the trimmings.

THOMAS'S FACE

4 Using the remaining black sugarpaste, roll out and cut a strip to cover the engine around Thomas's face. Colour 185g (6oz) modelling paste black. Using 30g (1oz), model Thomas's funnel, with two flattened circles on top, and fill the 'portholes', cab doors and windows with thinly rolled-out black modelling paste. Roll out 45g (1½oz) black paste, and cut out the cab roof, sticking in place with sugar glue. With the trimmings, model the two boiler supports for the top of the front chassis and cut two miniature circles for the buffers. Put aside to dry. Using the remaining grey sugarpaste, roll out and cut a 7.5cm (3 inch) circle for Thomas's face. Using the photograph, below, as a guide, model his face. Use the grey trimmings for the face padding on the underside, turn over and smooth

around to shape the nose and cheeks. Cut his smile with a knife and fill with a minute piece of white modelling paste, smoothing the paste into the corners with a damp paintbrush. Make two eyes with a little white and black modelling paste and cut out two triangular eyebrows. Re-cut the face with the circle cutter to remove excess paste, and stick in position.

WHEELS

5 Colour 60g (2oz) modelling paste blue. Using the 4.5cm (1¾inch) and 5cm (2 inch) circle cutters, cut out three hoops. Press in the centre of each inner circle with your finger as a cutting guide, then cut out the spokes. Stick the hoops around the spokes to make the wheels, then cut each wheel in half. With the trimmings, model six flattened balls and make six counterweights, each cut from a circle, then stick everything in position with a little sugar glue. Thinly roll out the remaining red modelling paste, and cut

out all the thin strips for the engine, sticking in place with sugar glue. Stick the dome on top. Stick two flattened red balls on to the front of the chassis for the buffer stems, then stick on the black buffers made earlier. Make a card template of the larger no. 1 outline on page 91, and cut out two red number ones. Stick in place on either side of the engine.

THE FAT CONTROLLER, SIR TOPHAM HATT

6 To make The Fat Controller, first colour 30g (1oz) modelling paste grey (using a little black colouring), 22g (¾ oz) yellow, and 15g (½ oz) flesh-coloured. Model two fat teardrop shapes for his shoes using 7g (¼oz) black modelling paste. Using all of the grey, make his trousers, then stick his trousers on to his shoes. With 22g (¾ oz) white modelling paste, model his top. Hollow out the

base so it sits neatly over his trousers, keeping a plump, well-rounded shape. Using 7g (¼oz) of the yellow, cut out the front of his waistcoat, indenting down the centre with a knife. Thinly roll out 15g (½oz) black modelling paste and cut out his jacket, collar and lapels, sticking in place with sugar glue. With another 15g (½oz), model his two arms, make his hat using a 2.5cm (1 inch) circle cutter for the brim, and model his tie. Make his head and two hands with the flesh-coloured modelling paste, and cut the top of his head flat so his hat sits straight. With a little of the flesh trimmings, model his triangular-shaped nose. Stick The Fat Controller alongside Thomas and leave to dry.

Thinly roll out a little of the remaining yellow and cut strips to edge the cab. Cut out hoops to edge the 'portholes' using the two smallest circle cutters. Cut out two yellow number ones using a template made from the smaller no. 1 outline on page 91. Use the remaining yellow to model the engine whistle. Model the coal pieces using the remaining black modelling paste. Stick all these items in place, then, when the cake is dry, draw in The Fat Controller's face and waistcoat buttons using a black food colouring pen. Dust his cheeks with a little red dusting powder.

on page 91.

Tip

Store the finished cake in a cardboard box in a warm dry room. NEVER store in the refrigerator; the atmosphere is damp and the cake will spoil.

Spot

A loveable puppy who gets up to all sorts of tricks, Spot is a favourite of all small children.

PARCELS

1 Trim the crust from the cake. To make the boxes, cut the cake into four squares, then cut one of the squares in half. Cut one of these in half again to make the two smallest boxes. Spread a layer of buttercream over the surface of each cake to help the sugarpaste stick. Roll out 875g (1¾lb) sugarpaste and cut out pieces to cover all the cakes by positioning each cake side down on to the sugarpaste and cutting round it. Roll out another 375g (12oz) sugarpaste and use to cover the cake board.

2 Colour 90g (3oz) sugarpaste mauve and roll out thinly. Stand one of the large cakes on its side, dampen with a lit-

tle sugar glue, then cover the cake completely with mauve sugarpaste. Colour 100g (3½oz) sugarpaste lilac. Thinly roll out 15g (½oz) and cut out small circles using the end of a no. 4 piping tube. Stick the lilac spots on the mauve parcel using a little sugar glue. Colour 155g (5oz) sugarpaste blue, 75g (2½oz) green, 75g (2½oz) red and the remainder pink. Using 60g (2oz) each of the blue and red, all of the green and pink, and the remaining lilac sugarpaste, thinly roll out and use to cover all the cakes. Reserve the green trimmings.

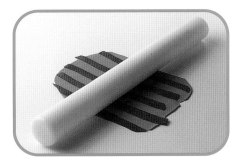

3 Colour 22g (¾oz) modelling paste dark pink, 45g (1½oz) pale yellow, 15g (½oz) black and 15g (½oz) orange, and with some of the green sugarpaste trimmings, thinly roll out and cut strips for the ribbons and bows. Use pieces of foam to support the loops in the bows whilst drying. Cut out a gift tag and bow shapes from the pale yellow modelling paste using the miniature bow cutter. (Reserve all the trimmings.) Stick everything in place using a little sugar glue. Position the cakes on the cake board. To make the striped wrapping paper, thinly roll out the remaining blue and red sugarpaste. Cut strips from the red and stick them on to the blue. (Reserve the red trimmings.) Using the rolling pin, roll

Tip
To avoid the paste 'pulling' when you cut it, use a sharp, plain-edged knife. Do not draw the blade through the paste, but cut cleanly downwards.

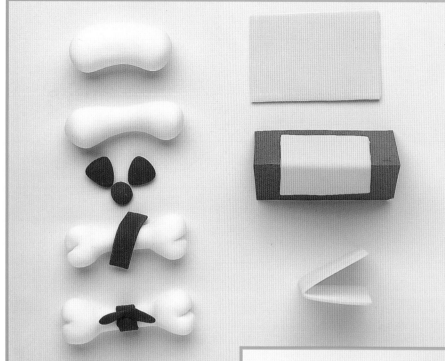

tip on the end of his tail, rolling together to join. With the black modelling paste trimmings, make his eyes and nose.

TO FINISH

6 When the cake is completely dry, draw the patterns on the cards and wrapping paper, and mark some writing on the gift tag, using a black food colouring pen. Place Spot in position.

over the 'wrapping paper' to inlay the stripes, then cut out an oblong and position on the cake board, lifting the corners and creating a tuck in the paste for a realistic effect.

SPOT'S BONE & CARDS

4 Using 7g (¼ oz) modelling paste, make Spot's bone (using the photograph, above, as a guide). Use the red sugarpaste trimmings to make the bow. Cut out one green and one pale yellow card using the reserved trimmings. Fold a square of paper at an angle to use as a former, and position the pale yellow card over it. Leave to dry completely before removing.

SPOT

5 To make Spot, colour 250g (8oz) modelling paste yellow and the remaining modelling paste brown. Model Spot's body first, using 140g (4½ oz). Use a small piece of foam to support the front legs whilst drying. Roll a ball for his head using 75g (2½ oz) paste, and cut his ears either side, shaping a rounded muzzle. Indent his smile using a knife, and dimple the corners using the tip of the no. 4 piping tube. Indent either side of

his nose with the tip of a cocktail stick. Stick his head in place using a little sugar glue. With the remaining yellow modelling paste, make Spot's back legs and tail. Mark his paws with a knife. Using a little brown modelling paste, make his spot and the tip of his tail, hollowing out the base. Stick his spot on his side, and the

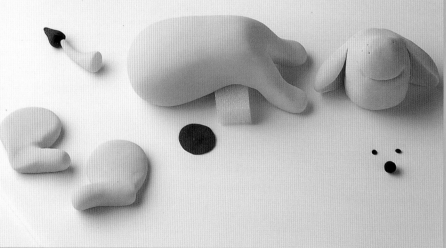

OLD BEAR™

Well known for their adventures in the playroom, Old Bear and Little Bear are two much-loved characters from Jane Hissey's delightful children's story books.

MATERIALS

20cm (8 inch) square cake
30cm (12 inch) square cake board
1.25kg (2 ½ lb) sugarpaste (rolled fondant)
410g (13oz) buttercream
700g (1lb 6 ½ oz) modelling paste
100g (3 ½ oz) royal icing
brown, black, golden brown, dark green, peach, red, cream and blue food colouring pastes
cool boiled water
sugar glue
black food colouring pen

☆

EQUIPMENT

large and small rolling pins
sharp knife
long ruler
cocktail sticks (toothpicks)
medium paintbrush
foam sheet
greaseproof paper piping bags
nos. 1 and 2 plain piping tubes (tips)

Tip
To help support Old Bear, insert a sugar stick (see page 13) or a piece of raw dried spaghetti inside his body, then gently press on his head.

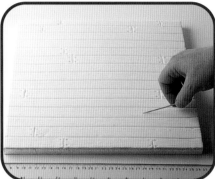

BOARD

1 Roll out 440g (14oz) sugarpaste and use to cover the cake board. Using a long ruler, indent lines across the board to represent floorboards. With a cocktail stick, scratch on the lines for the wood-grain effect and indent for the joins and nails. Dilute some brown food colouring paste with cool boiled water. Using a medium paintbrush, paint a colourwash over the floorboards, letting the colour run into the gaps and scratched wood-grain to make them stand out (see page 12). Put aside to dry.

large box layer 1	small box
large box layer 2	bag

BOXES

2 Trim the crust from the cake and cut the cake as shown in the diagram (above). To make the large box, sandwich the two large cakes together with butter-cream, then stand upright. Spread a thin layer of buttercream over the surface of each cake to help the sugarpaste stick.

3 Roll out 410g (13oz) sugarpaste. Cut a straight edge, then lift the paste and use it to cover the large box, aligning the straight edge of the paste along the top and side edges at the front of the

box, leaving the front uncovered. Trim around the base, and pinch along each edge to square off. Mark the box folds on the back using a knife (see back view of box, page 61). Thinly roll out 60g (2oz) sugarpaste and cut a piece to cover the front of the box. Position the cake on the cake board. Dilute a little black food colouring with some cool boiled water and paint over the front of the box for

the opening. Measure the box opening, then thinly roll out 100g (3½oz) modelling paste and cut four box flaps to fit. Bend the corners and edges of each and wrinkle the surfaces, then place on a foam sheet to dry. Roll out 200g (6½oz) sugarpaste and cover the medium-sized cake for the small box, pinching the edges to square off as before. To mark the small box lid, indent on each side

using a ruler. Dilute a little golden brown food colouring paste with some water, and paint a thin coat over the two boxes and the box flaps. Set aside to dry.

BAG

4 Roll out 140g (4½oz) sugarpaste and use to cover the smallest piece of cake completely, pressing the paste around the back and smoothing the joins closed. Make the bag flap using the sugarpaste trimmings, sticking in place with sugar glue. Dilute a little dark green food colouring paste with some water. Stipple the colour on to the bag using the paintbrush (see page 13). Colour 60g (2oz) modelling paste brown. Using half, roll out and cut strips for the bag handle, trim and straps. Press the tip of a cocktail stick into the straps to make holes.

OLD BEAR & LITTLE BEAR

5 Colour 280g (9oz) modelling paste very pale peach. To make Old Bear, model his tummy first, using 100g (3½oz) paste, then model his head with 60g (2oz), shaping a pointed muzzle. Make Old Bear's arms with 30g (1oz) paste, and his legs with 45g (1½oz). With the remaining pale peach, make Old Bear's two ears and Little Bear's chest, head, ears and arms. Shape two balls for Little Bear's feet. Colour 30g (1oz) modelling paste red and use half to model Little Bear's trousers. Assemble Old Bear and Little Bear together in their pose, sticking with sugar glue. Indent the seam lines from Old Bear's muzzle to his ears using a knife. Colour 75g (2½oz) of the royal icing cream. Using a piping bag with a

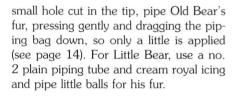

(see page 14).

small hole cut in the tip, pipe Old Bear's fur, pressing gently and dragging the piping bag down, so only a little is applied (see page 14). For Little Bear, use a no. 2 plain piping tube and cream royal icing and pipe little balls for his fur.

BOX FLAPS, BOOKS & LITTLE BEAR'S BAG

6 Secure the dry box flaps in position at the front of the box with dabs of royal icing. Using 170g (5½ oz) modelling paste, cut out different-sized blocks for the book pages, marking around the edges with a knife, and thinly roll out and cut oblongs for the newspaper, sticking in place with a little sugar glue. Colour pieces of the remaining modelling paste dark blue, dark green and dark cream. Using this and the remaining red and dark brown paste, make all the book covers and Little Bear's bag.

TO FINISH

7 Colour tiny amounts of the modelling paste trimmings medium brown and black, and make Little Bear's button eyes, sticking a minute white dot of paste on each eye to highlight. Stipple some diluted golden brown food colouring over Old Bear's fur and paint his thread-bare feet. When the cake is dry, draw the print on to the books and newspaper using a black food colouring pen. Position Old Bear and Little Bear on the cake board. Colour the remaining royal icing black. Using a no. 1 plain piping tube, pipe small lines to look like stitches for Old Bear's eyes, nose, mouth, paws and feet, and Little Bear's nose and mouth.

© *Peyo* - 1997

Licensed through I.M.P.S. (Brussels)

Make this cake for a birthday treat, but be careful, watch out for little hands that have been sent by the evil sorcerer Gargamel!

MATERIALS

1 litre (2 pint/5 cup) and 750ml
(1¼ pint/3 cup) bowl cakes
(page 84)
20cm (8 inch) round cake board
375g (12oz) buttercream
1kg (2lb) sugarpaste (rolled fondant)
280g (9oz) modelling paste
yellow, mauve, red, black, golden
brown, blue and green food
colouring pastes
sugar glue
black food colouring pen

☆

EQUIPMENT

sharp knife
large rolling pin
2.5cm (1 inch) square cutter
card for templates
scissors
miniature heart cutter
large star piping tube (tip)

HOUSE

1 Trim the crust from each cake, leaving the tops rounded where they have risen. Slightly hollow out the top of the large cake so it will sit neatly on top of the small cake. Trim the sides of the large cake to shape the roof, and trim around the base of the roof to round off, shaping it into a curve at the front for above the doorway. Cut out the doorway in the small cake.

2 Cut the large cake horizontally into two layers and sandwich together again with buttercream. Spread a thin layer of buttercream over the surface of both cakes to help the sugarpaste stick. Colour 315g (10oz) sugarpaste yellow. Roll out 280g (9oz) and use to cover the small cake, smoothing the paste into the doorway. (Reserve the trimmings.) Cut

out two windows either side of the doorway using a 2.5cm (1 inch) square cutter.

3 Colour 410g (13oz) sugarpaste mauve. Roll out 375g (12oz) and use to cover the large cake, smoothing around the base and underneath. Assemble the cakes, one on top of the other, on the cake board. Make a card

Tip
Wear plastic gloves when kneading the colours into paste as the food colouring might stain your hands.

62

template of the roof marking using the outline on page 93. Colour 45g (1½ oz) sugarpaste red. Roll out thinly and cut out the shape, using the template as a guide. Model an additional tiny red marking for the roof with some trimmings. Stick both pieces in place using a little sugar glue.

4 Colour 45g (1½oz) modelling paste black. Roll out thinly and cut out pieces to fill each window. For the inside of the roof balcony, roll out and cut a 4cm (1¾ inch) wedge of paste, that is thick at the top and thin at the base, shaping it so the thick end becomes the pointed top and the thin end the base, so it will sit in a vertical position against the sloping roof. Reserve the black trimmings. Stick the black balcony piece in position with sugar glue. Make a card template of the balcony roof using the outline on page 93. Colour 75g (2½oz) modelling paste golden brown. Using 45g (1½ oz), cut out the base of the balcony and a hand-rail to fit over the black inside of the balcony, and mark lines on them with a knife to create a woodgrain effect (see page 12). Model three golden brown balls. Roll out some more golden brown paste and cut out the balcony roof. Stick in position, then mark lines with a knife as before. Assemble the balcony, sticking with sugar glue. Using the remaining golden brown paste, make the door, door handle, roof supports for above the doorway, and two window-sills, marking each with a knife as before.

With the trimmings, make four stalks for the toadstools and put aside. Cut an arched window in the door and fill with a little of the black modelling paste trimmings. Thinly roll out the yellow sugarpaste trimmings and cut out the pathway, marking lines in the surface with a knife. Stick little flattened balls of paste over the surface for stones.

5 Colour 60g (2oz) modelling paste pale grey (with a little black colouring). Make the chimney using 45g (1½ oz), cutting a square of paste for the top. Trim the side of the chimney to fit against the roof. Stick in place with a little sugar glue and hold for a few moments until secure. Make two steps with the remaining grey and stick on the

door threshold. Colour the grey trimmings a slightly darker shade and model flattened balls for the chimney, sticking in place with a little sugar glue. Colour 22g (¾oz) modelling paste red. Thinly roll out 7g (¼oz) and cut out two sets of curtains for the windows, pleating them as you stick them in place. With the remaining mauve modelling paste, make the window shutters. Mark a line down the centre of each with a knife, and cut out a heart in each using a miniature heart cutter. Add woodgrain effects as before. Stick in place using a little sugar glue.

SMURFS

6 Colour 15g (½ oz) modelling paste blue. Set aside 7g (¼oz) for Smurfette, then split the remainder into three equally sized pieces. Use one piece to model a head, ears and nose for Papa Smurf. Make his hat using 7g (¼ oz) red modelling paste, hollowing the base so it sits neatly on his head. Make flattened pieces of white modelling paste for his beard and two tiny eyes and eyebrows. Using a minute amount of black modelling paste, model two pupils for his eyes. Make six more pupils and put aside. Stick Papa Smurf in position at the window. Make two Smurfs with white hats for the other window using the other two pieces of blue modelling paste.

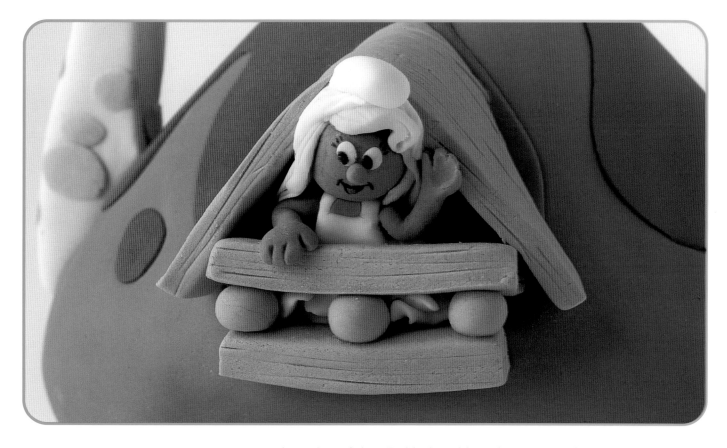

SMURFETTE

7 First model Smurfette's dress with a square neck using 7g (¼oz) white modelling paste, pinching a frill around the base. Stick to the inside of the balcony. Using the remaining blue modelling paste, make her neck, arms and hands, head and a small nose. Make her hat and two eyes using 7g (¼oz) white modelling paste, and stick the black

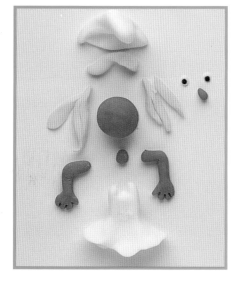

pupils in place. Colour 7g (¼ oz) modelling paste yellow and stick small pieces around her face for her hair, marking lines with a cocktail stick. When all the Smurfs are dry, draw in their smiles and grins with a black food colouring pen. Stick a minute amount of red modelling paste on to the smile of Papa Smurf and Smurfette for their tongues.

TO FINISH

8 Colour the remaining sugarpaste green. Roll out pieces and stick on to the cake board. Create a grass effect by repeatedly pressing the tip of a large star piping tube into the paste. With the remaining red and white modelling paste, make the tops of the toadstools and stick

them on to the stalks made earlier. Position on the grass.

NODDY ™

Instead of tearing around Toy Town in his little yellow car, Noddy will give Big-Ears a lift and make a stop instead at your child's birthday party.

BOARD & CAR

1 Colour 315g (10oz) sugarpaste lilac. Roll out and use to cover the cake board. Crimp the edge of the cake board using a crimping tool, and set aside to dry. Trim the crust from the cake, keeping the top rounded where the cake has risen. To shape the car, trim the front and back to round off, keeping the bonnet high and rounded. Trim the top from the bonnet to slope down to the centre, then trim level to the back. Trim out the seat area from the centre of the car. Trim the edge from around the base of the car

so the sugarpaste will tuck under neatly. Spread the cake with a layer of buttercream to help the sugarpaste stick. Colour 625g (1¼lb) sugarpaste yellow. Roll out and cover the car completely. Position on the cake board. Using the back of a knife, mark the lines on the bonnet and for the car doors.

2 Colour 345g (11oz) sugarpaste pale grey (using a little black colouring). Split into five equal pieces and make the wheels, marking the tyre lines with a knife. Stick in place, with the spare tyre on the back. Colour the remaining sugarpaste red. Split into four equal pieces and make the four wheel arches. Colour 22g (¾oz) modelling paste yellow. Roll out 15g (½oz) and cut out five circles with a 2cm (¾ inch) circle cutter for the centres of the wheels. Roll five balls from the yellow trimmings, and stick in place. Roll two tiny yellow balls to go on the folded-down soft-top of the car, and put aside. (Reserve the yellow trimmings.) Colour 15g (½oz) modelling paste black.

MATERIALS

23x13cm (9x5 inch) oblong cake
(page 84)
25cm (10 inch) round cake board
1.6kg (3lb 2oz) sugarpaste (rolled
fondant)
185g (6oz) buttercream
500g (1lb) modelling paste
lilac, yellow, black, red, pink,
mauve, flesh, blue and brown food
colouring pastes
clear alcohol (gin or vodka) or cool
boiled water
sugar glue
black food colouring pen
pink dusting powder (petal
dust/blossom tint)

☆

EQUIPMENT

large and small rolling pins
sharp knife
crimping tool
2cm (¾ inch), 2.5cm (1 inch) and
7.5cm (3 inch) circle cutters
miniature teardrop/petal cutter
fine paintbrush
ruler
card for templates
no. 4 plain piping tube (tip)
pieces of foam

Roll out half and cut out a circle using a 2.5cm (1 inch) cutter for the steering wheel. Use the miniature teardrop/petal cutter to cut out the centre areas of the steering wheel. For the windscreen, push the end of a paintbrush down into the car about 1cm (½ inch) in depth on either side to make two holes. Measure the distance between them exactly. Roll out the remaining black modelling paste and cut the windscreen frame to fit. Put the steering wheel and windscreen aside to dry completely. Make a card template for the front grille (see page 90). Using 90g (3oz) white modelling paste, cut out the front grille (using the template), and model all the lights, marking the lines with a knife and the indented circles with the end of a no. 4 piping tube. Make two bumpers and door handles, and a 'cap' for the front grille, and stick in place.

3 Colour 30g (1oz) modelling paste pink. To make the car seat, roll out and cut a circle using a 7.5cm (3 inch) circle cutter. Cut the circle in two, making one half slightly larger than the other. Using the larger half circle, indent radiating lines with the back of a knife (see illustration, above right).

Press down with your fingers along the top edge to scallop, then stick in place with a little sugar glue. Colour 90g (3oz) modelling paste dark mauve. Make a card template for the soft-top (see page 90). Roll out the mauve paste, making

one end thick and the other thin. Cut out the base of the soft-top using the template, with the back on the thicker end of the paste. Cut out the half circle from the centre of the front using the 7.5cm (3 inch) circle cutter. Mark the folds along the back and around the sides using a knife. Cut out the top of the soft-top in the same way, but do not make it quite so thick, and position on top of the base, using a little sugar glue. Stick on to the car and add the two tiny yellow balls made earlier.

NODDY

4 First colour 60g (2oz) modelling paste red, 60g (2oz) flesh-coloured, 60g (2oz) blue and 7g (¼ oz) brown. Using just under half of the red, model Noddy's top by rolling a ball and flattening it slightly. Cut either side for the arms. Smooth the edges and gently twist the arms down, flattening the ends. Bend halfway along the arms for the elbows. Slot Noddy's top into the car seat, leaving enough room for Big-Ears, sticking in place with a little sugar glue. Model two balls for the sleeve cuffs using some of the red trimmings, and stick in place. Make Noddy's scarf and model his hat bell using the remaining yel-

low modelling paste. Using just under half of the flesh-coloured modelling paste, make Noddy's head, nose, ears and hands. Stick in place, with Noddy's hands holding the steering wheel. Mark his smile using the curve of the miniature teardrop/petal cutter, and dimple the corners with the tip of the no. 4 piping tube. Model Noddy's hat next, using half of the blue modelling paste. Slightly hollow out the base and stick in place using foam pieces to support the head and hat whilst drying. Stick his yellow bell at the end of his hat. Make Noddy's eyes from tiny circles of white, blue and black paste trimmings, and make red dots for his scarf. Put aside a minute amount of brown modelling paste for later, then model Noddy's hair by cutting a circle of brown paste into a five-pointed star shape, twisting the points and indenting with a cocktail stick. Stick in place, and add two extra pieces of 'hair' above Noddy's ears.

BIG-EARS

5 To make Big-Ears, first model a fat teardrop shape for his body using 22g (¾ oz) white modelling paste. Cut two red stripes for his jumper. With the remaining blue, roll and cut out his jacket to fit around the back of his body and just cover his sides, and make the jacket lapels and sleeves. Stick in position next to Noddy in the car seat. With the remaining flesh-coloured paste, make his head, nose, rounded cheeks, pointed ears and hands. Mark his smile in the same way as Noddy's. Model Big-Ears' hat in the same way as Noddy's, using the remaining red modelling paste and twisting the point upwards. Stick small balls of white modelling paste on to Big-

Ears for his hair and beard, then press in with the end of a paintbrush to 'curl'. Make his eyes in the same way as Noddy's but using the remaining brown modelling paste instead of blue.

TO FINISH

6 Dilute a little black food colouring paste with clear alcohol. Lightly paint on to the grille, bumper, door handles and lights to give a shiny 'silver' paint effect. Draw eyelashes and eyebrows on Noddy and Big-Ears using a black food colouring pen. To give Noddy and Big-Ears a blush, dust a little pink dusting powder on to their cheeks and on Big-Ears' nose. Carefully slot the windscreen in place.

Tip To help hold the heads in place, push a sugar stick (see page 13) or length of raw dried spaghetti down into each body, then gently push on the heads.

MATERIALS

two 1 litre (2 pint/5 cup) bowl-shaped cakes or spherical cake (page 85)
25cm (10 inch) round cake board
1.25kg (2½lb) sugarpaste (rolled fondant)
125g (4oz) modelling paste
280g (9oz) buttercream
90g (3oz) royal icing
navy blue, blue, green, brown, flesh and red food colouring pastes
sugar glue
black food colouring pen

☆

EQUIPMENT

large and small rolling pins
sharp knife
small star cutter
atlas for reference
fine paintbrush
cake smoother
miniature circle cutter
piece of foam

When choosing ribbon for the cake board banding, remember you need a slightly thicker width if you cover the cake board with sugarpaste (rolled fondant).

WHERE'S WALLY?

For Wally/Waldo-Watchers everywhere, it's a game, it's a cult, it's a worldwide obsession, and now ... it's a cake!

BOARD

1 Colour 315g (10oz) sugarpaste navy blue. Roll out and use to cover the cake board. Use a small star cutter to cut stars out of the sugarpaste. Roll out 15g (½oz) white modelling paste to the same depth as the cut-out stars. Cut out white stars to fill the spaces in the navy sugarpaste. Leave the stars for a few minutes before slotting into place.

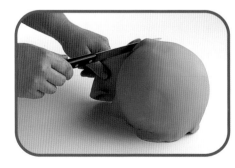

GLOBE

2 Trim the crusts from both cakes. Sandwich the two cakes together with buttercream, then spread a thin layer of buttercream over the surface of

the cake to help the sugarpaste stick. Colour 875g (1¾ lb) sugarpaste blue. Roll out and use to cover the cake completely. Smooth around the base and pull up the pleat at the back. Cut away the pleat, then rub the join closed. Position the cake on the cake board.

3 Colour the remaining sugarpaste green. Using an atlas as a guide, model simple land shapes. As each piece of land is made, stick it in place with a little sugar glue, then, using a cake smoother, work over the surface of the cake to inlay.

WALLY/WALDO

4 Colour 45g (1½oz) modelling paste navy blue. To make Wally's trousers, model a sausage shape, then make a cut

three-quarters of the way along it to separate the legs. Smooth the edges to
round off, and cut the bottom of each leg
straight. Pinch halfway along for the
knees. Bend into a sitting position, then
stick in place on the globe with sugar
glue. Colour 7g (¼ oz) modelling paste
pale brown. Make Wally's walking stick
and set aside to dry, then model his
shoes, indenting around them with a
knife to mark the soles. To make Wally's
jumper, roll 30g (1oz) white modelling
paste into a ball and slightly flatten it. Cut
one sleeve either side. Twist each sleeve
down to lengthen, and smooth the
ridges. Hollow out the base and stick in
position over Wally's trousers. Colour 7g
(¼oz) modelling paste flesh-coloured.
Make Wally's head, ears, nose and
hands. Stick in position, then indent
Wally's grin by pushing in a miniature
circle cutter at an angle. To make Wally's
hair, colour 7g (¼ oz) modelling
paste dark brown. Attach
small flattened pieces of
brown paste to the back
of Wally's head and
mark with a knife. For
his quiff, roll tiny pointed sausages of brown
paste and assemble
on his forehead.
With 7g (¼ oz)
white paste,
model Wally's
hat and two

circles for his glasses.
Colour the remaining
modelling paste red
and roll it out thinly.
Cut strips for Wally's
jumper and hat, and
stick in position
with sugar glue. Roll
a ball with the trim-
mings for his hat
bobble. Stick his
walking stick in
place.

TO FINISH

5 When the cake is dry, draw in
Wally's eyes and glasses' frame using
a black food colouring pen. For the
clouds, spread a little royal icing on the
cake and stipple using a piece of foam.

Paddington™

The marmalade sandwiches will miraculously disappear when Paddington is put centre-stage on the birthday-party table.

MATERIALS

25cm (10 inch) square cake
20cm (8 inch) square cake board
1.65kg (3¼ lb) sugarpaste (rolled fondant)
375g (12oz) buttercream
brown, golden brown, blue, yellow, red and black food colouring pastes
sugar glue
black food colouring pen

☆

EQUIPMENT

sharp knife
large rolling pin
ruler
13cm (5 inch), 10cm (4 inch),
7.5cm (3 inch) and 5cm (2 inch)
circle cutters
fine paintbrush
no. 4 plain piping tube (tip)

Tip

After the buttercream is spread on the surface of the cake, it might begin to set before you apply the sugarpaste. If so, simply rework the buttercream with a knife or apply a little more.

BOARD & CAKE

1 Roll out 280g (9oz) sugarpaste and use to cover the cake board. Put aside to dry. Trim the crust from the cake. Cut an oblong for the suitcase measuring 10x14cm (4x5½ inches) from one corner. Position the four circle cutters on the remaining cake, and cut out the circles of cake. Arrange them one on top of the other with the largest at the base.

2 Trim the edges from around the tower of circle cakes, and trim the base at the back to round off Paddington's bottom. Sandwich the circle cakes together with buttercream, then

spread a thin layer of buttercream over the surface of all the cakes, including the oblong, to help the sugarpaste stick.

SUITCASE

3 Colour 280g (9oz) sugarpaste brown. Roll out and use to cover the suitcase, marking a line around the sides for the opening with the back of a knife. Colour the trimmings a darker brown and make the suitcase trims and handle. Stick in place with the handle on the back of the suitcase. Position Paddington on top of the suitcase with his bottom in line with the back of the suitcase. Place on the cake board.

PADDINGTON

4 Colour 170g (5½ oz) sugarpaste golden brown. Split a 75g (2½ oz) piece in two and model Paddington's

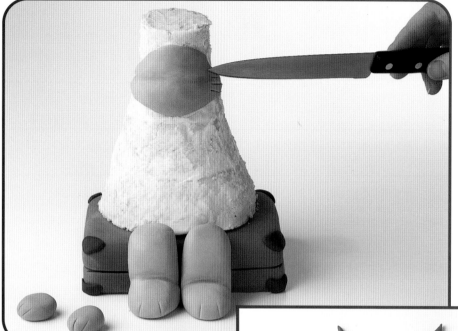

5 Colour 625g (1 ¼ lb) sugarpaste blue. Roll out 410g (13oz) and cut an oblong measuring 13x44cm (5x17 inches) for Paddington's coat. Wrap around the back of Paddington, smoothing the paste around his body, and trim the join at the front for the coat opening. Trim excess from around his knees. Indent the pleats using the end of a paintbrush. Model Paddington's sleeves using 140g (4 ½ oz) blue paste split in two, and use some more blue to model his hood. Roll out the remainder and cut out the collar, sleeve straps and strap for the back, indenting with the tip of a no. 4 plain piping tube to represent buttons. Cut two straps to go between the toggles on the front. Colour 7g (¼ oz) sugarpaste yellow and make four toggles. Stick everything in place using a little sugar glue.

legs and feet, slightly indenting with a knife. Using 22g (¾ oz), again split into two and model his two paws, indenting as before. Make his face and snout using the remaining golden brown sugarpaste, and press in position, smoothing the top and sides in line with the surface of the cake. Using a knife, cut the fur slightly, flicking it up on either side of his head.

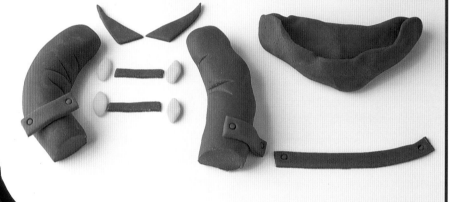

Indent pleats in the back of Paddington's coat with the end of a paintbrush.

6 Colour 250g (8oz) sugarpaste red. Using the photograph, below, as a guide, model Paddington's hat. Hollow out the base to fit on top of the cake, and turn up the hat brim, sticking in place with a little sugar glue. Mark the pleats with the end of a paintbrush. Colour the remaining sugarpaste black. Model Paddington's eyes and nose, and cut a strip for his hat. When the cake is dry, draw in Paddington's smile with a black food colouring pen.

BEATRIX POTTER
PETER RABBIT
& FRIENDS™

The delightful animal stories written and illustrated by Beatrix Potter have captured the imagination of children throughout the world for four generations. Here are just some of her enchanting characters modelled in sugar.

MATERIALS

20cm (8 inch) hexagonal cake
30cm (12 inch) hexagonal cake board
1.25kg (2 ½ lb) sugarpaste (rolled fondant)
410g (13oz) buttercream
30g (1oz) royal icing
185g (6oz) modelling paste
brown, golden brown, blue, green, red, black, yellow, pink and chestnut food colouring pastes
clear alcohol (gin or vodka) or cool boiled water
sugar glue

☆

EQUIPMENT

large and small rolling pins
sharp knife
greaseproof paper piping bag
nos. 1 and 4 plain piping tubes (tips)
greaseproof paper
cocktail sticks (toothpicks)
fine paintbrushes and medium hard bristle paintbrush
sharp, pointed scissors
bone modelling tool
colour mixing palette

Tip

Paint scenes and figures first and leave to dry before positioning on the cake and board. For tips on paint effects, see pages 11–13.

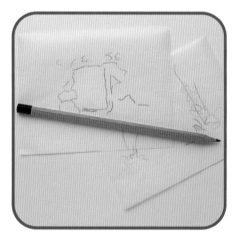

BOARD & CAKE

1 Roll out 500g (1lb) sugarpaste and use to cover the cake board. Leave to dry. Trim the crust from the cake, then split and fill with buttercream. Spread a thin layer of buttercream over the surface of the cake to help the sugarpaste stick. Position on the cake board. Roll out the remaining sugarpaste and use to cover the cake. Using the royal icing and a no. 1 piping tube, pipe a snail's trail around the base of the cake. Trace the side design outlines (pages 90–91) on to greaseproof paper. Carefully scribe the designs on to the sides of the cake using a cocktail stick.

PETER RABBIT

2 To make Peter Rabbit, model a teardrop shape using 7g (¼oz) modelling paste for his body. Split another 7g (¼oz) in two. With one piece, model Peter's tail, two feet and hands, then make his head, shaping a slightly pointed muzzle and his two ears, and indenting down the centre of each ear using the end of a paintbrush. Thinly roll out the other piece of paste and cut a strip for Peter's jacket, sticking in place around his back with the join at the front. Using the trimmings, model his sleeves, sticking in place with his hands using sugar glue, and make his nose and

two minute balls for his eyes. Before sticking his eyes in place, press the end of a paintbrush into his face to indent. Using another 7g (¼ oz) paste, model a spade, cutting the handle open by pressing the tip of a no. 1 plain piping tube into the top repeatedly. Make the robin and model small flattened balls of paste for the earth. Make a radish and leaves, frilling the edges of each leaf by rolling a cocktail stick around the edges.

JEMIMA PUDDLE-DUCK

3 Model Jemima's body using 15g (½ oz) modelling paste, bending up her tail and neck, rounding her head and smoothing her beak to a point. Split a 7g (¼ oz) piece of modelling paste in two. Thinly roll out one piece and cut out a shawl to fit over her back, joining at the front. With the other piece, model Jemima's webbed feet and stick a flattened circle on the back of her head for the back of her bonnet. Thinly roll out the trimmings and cut a strip for the base of the bonnet and the bonnet rim. Stick in place with sugar glue and smooth upwards, then cut two tiny bonnet ribbons.

MRS TIGGY-WINKLE

4 Roll 15g (½ oz) paste into a ball for Mrs Tiggy-winkle's body. Roll another ball, using 7g (¼ oz) paste, for her head and shape a pointed muzzle. Mark lines from her nose outwards around her face and indent for her eyes using the end of a paintbrush. Using 15g (½ oz) paste, model two sleeves and a dress ruffle at the back, then thinly roll out the trimmings and cut out an apron and

handkerchief, indenting the pattern with a cocktail stick. Model a bow for Mrs Tiggy-winkle's back and make her cap, frilling the edge by pressing the end of a paintbrush along the edge. 'Snip' her prickles with the tip of a pointed pair of scissors, and tease them up using a damp paintbrush. Model two minute balls for Mrs Tiggy-winkle's eyes, and make her nose, indenting nostrils with a cocktail stick.

SQUIRREL NUTKIN

5 Split a 7g (¼ oz) piece of modelling paste in half. Use one half to model the branch on which Squirrel Nutkin is sitting by rolling a sausage shape and thinning it at one end. Make cuts for the smaller branches and twist gently to lengthen and shape. Mark lines with a knife to create a woodgrain appearance (see page 12). Cut the branch in two to leave room for Squirrel Nutkin, and stick in position on the board with the branches up against the side of the cake. (This is the only modelled piece that is stuck in place before painting.) Model the other piece of paste into a teardrop shape for the squirrel's body. Split another 7g (¼ oz) paste in two and use one piece to model a small head with a rounded muzzle. Indent hollows for his eyes with the end of a paintbrush, and shape two pointed ears. Using trimmings, model the squirrel's arms and feet (marking with a knife), two minute eyes, a nose and the three nuts. Use the other piece of paste to model his bushy tail, marking lines with a knife, and stick on to his back curving the top of his tail around.

BENJAMIN BUNNY & FLOPSY

6 To make the Benjamin Bunny scene, first split a 22g (¾oz) piece of modelling paste into three. Using two pieces, model teardrop shapes for the bodies of Benjamin Bunny and Flopsy, then with the other piece model the sack. Split another 15g (½oz) piece in half. Using one piece, thinly roll out and cut a strip of paste for Benjamin Bunny's jacket, wrapping it around his back with the join at his neck. Model his head, indenting hollows for the eyes with the end of a paintbrush, and model his sleeves, ears, eyes, nose, tail, hands and feet. Using the other piece of paste, thinly roll and cut out Flopsy's apron with a collar at the back, and model her head, ears, eyes, nose, tail, arms and feet.

MRS TITTLEMOUSE

7 To make Mrs Tittlemouse, model a teardrop shape for her body, using 7g (¼oz) modelling paste. Split a further 7g (¼oz) piece in two, and with one piece make her head, indenting hollows with the end of a paintbrush for her eyes. Model two minute eyes, two tiny feet and her tail, and make her ears using a bone modelling tool to indent the centres. Using the other piece of paste, make two sleeves with a tiny hand at the end of each, and add an extra 'bustle' of paste to her dress around the back, finishing it with a bow.

JEREMY FISHER

8 To make the Jeremy Fisher scene, first make the lily pad he is sitting on. Using 7g (¼oz) modelling paste, thinly roll out and cut the lily pad, frilling the edge by rolling a cocktail stick over the surface. Using the trimmings, make the fish and the worm, and roll very thin sausage shapes to make the fishing-rod and line. Lay the fishing-rod flat to dry. To make Jeremy Fisher, model his body by rolling 7g (¼oz) modelling paste into a ball. With a further 7g (¼oz) paste, make his legs, turning up the ends for his feet. Model his sleeves, hands, two flattened balls for his eyes, and his head, marking his wide grin with a knife. When sticking Jeremy's top hand in place, push the tip of a cocktail stick into the palm to make a hole the same thickness as the fishing rod so that it will slot in easily when dry.

PAINTING

9 Using food colouring pastes diluted with alcohol, paint all the designs on the sides of the cake, and the area in the centre top for Peter Rabbit. Paint all the figures. (See pages 11–13 for information on painting effects.) When everything is dry, arrange all the figures on and around the cake in their respective 'scenes', securing with sugar glue.

MATERIALS

20cm (8 inch) square cake
20x30cm (8x12 inch) oblong cake board
1.75kg (3½lb) sugarpaste (rolled fondant)
375g (12oz) buttercream
440g (14oz) modelling paste
blue, red, yellow, lime green, black, orange and green food colouring pastes
sugar glue
black food colouring pen

☆

EQUIPMENT

large and small rolling pins
sharp knife
fine paintbrush
2.5cm (1 inch) and 5cm (2 inch) circle cutters

Tip

When the sugarpaste is dry, polish the surface with your hands to remove excess icing (confectioners') sugar and to give a sheen.

MR. MEN
by Roger Hargreaves

Here are some of the adorable characters from the Mr. Men, but thank goodness Mr. Greedy isn't here or all the cake would be gobbled up!

BOARD & CAKE

1 Colour 375g (12oz) sugarpaste blue. Roll out and use to cover the cake board, then put aside to dry. Cut the crust from the cake. Cut the cake in half and half again to make four equally sized square cakes. Put one square cake aside for Mr. Strong. Cut the corners from the remaining cakes, then trim to round off. To make Mr. Tickle a taller, more oval shape, cut a layer in one round cake and sandwich back together with buttercream. Spread a thin layer of buttercream over the surface of each cake to help the sugarpaste stick.

MR. STRONG

2 To make Mr. Strong, first colour 375g (12oz) sugarpaste red. Roll out and cover the sides of the square cake by placing each side down on to the rolled-

out sugarpaste and cutting round. Using a little sugar glue to stick the edges together, smooth the joins closed. Carefully position Mr. Strong on the centre of the cake board. Colour 90g (3oz) modelling paste red. Using half, make Mr. Strong's hands and feet. Put his hands aside and stick his feet in place with a little sugar glue.

MR. HAPPY

3 Colour 315g (10oz) sugarpaste yellow. To make Mr. Happy, roll out the yellow paste and cover a round cake completely. Pull up a pleat at the back, cut away, then smooth the join closed. Position Mr.

Happy on top of Mr. Strong, sticking with sugar glue. Colour 90g (3oz) modelling paste yellow. Using half, make Mr. Happy's feet and hands, again sticking in position with sugar glue.

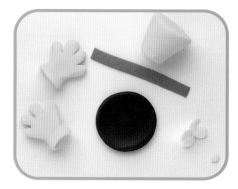

MR. FUNNY

4 Colour 315g (10oz) sugarpaste lime green. To make Mr. Funny, roll out the lime green paste and cover a round cake as before. Stick in position on the cake board, pressed up against Mr. Strong. Stick on two balls of lime green sugarpaste for his

arms, using some of the trimmings. Colour 30g (1oz) modelling paste black. To make the hat rims, thinly roll out the black paste and cut three large circles with a 5cm (2 inch) cutter, and one small circle with a 2.5cm (1 inch) cutter, indenting the centre of each. With the trimmings, model eight oval-shaped eyes and two tiny oval-shaped eyes. Put aside to dry. Using the remaining yellow modelling paste, make Mr. Funny's two gloves, hollowing the base of each to fit over his arms, and model his hat and the flower centre. Using 30g (1oz) white modelling paste, model two shoes, cutting off the end of each. With the trimmings, model a fat teardrop shape to make the flower, and press the end of a paintbrush into the rounded end. Make four cuts with a knife, then remove the paintbrush and open up the cuts, shaping the four petals. Colour 22g (¾ oz) modelling paste blue. Model the hats for Mr. Tickle and Mr. Small, sticking them on to the hat rims, and thinly roll out and cut Mr. Funny's hat band. Assemble Mr. Funny's hat on his head using sugar glue. Using 7g (¼oz) of the remaining red modelling paste, make Mr. Funny's nose, then roll a ball, cut it in half and stick on to the toes of his shoes.

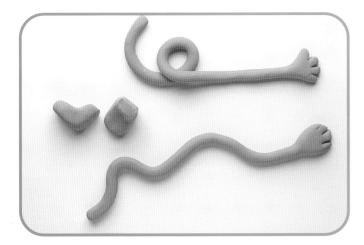

MR. TICKLE

5 Colour the remaining sugarpaste orange, roll out and cover the remaining cake with the buttercreamed layer, as before. Position on the cake board, sticking with sugar glue. Cut out Mr. Tickle's smile from the centre and fill with 7g (¼ oz) white modelling paste. Colour 125g (4oz) modelling paste orange. Using 30g (1oz), model his feet. Split the remaining piece exactly in half and roll two long sausage shapes, keeping the end of

each rounded. Slightly flatten each rounded end and make three cuts, then shape the fingers. Stick Mr. Tickle's hat on his head. Colour 22g (¾ oz) modelling paste dark green and make Mr. Strong's hat, sticking in place on his hat rim. Stick the hat in position in Mr. Tickle's hand.

MR. SMALL

6 To make Mr. Small, model a ball using 30g (1oz) of the remaining red modelling paste. With the remaining red, make his two hands and feet. Assemble on the cake board with his hat. Stick all the eyes in place using sugar glue. When the cake is dry, draw on all the smiles, eye surrounds, teeth and shoe laces using a black food colouring pen. Stick Mr. Strong's hands in place.

Tip To support the hands, insert a sugar stick (see page 13) inside.

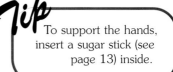

Cake Quantities Chart

Cake designs	Sooty (page 18)	Peanuts (page 26) The Wind in the Willows (page 29) Forever Friends (page 42) Paddington (page 73)	Country Companions (page 22) The Smurfs (page 62)
Bakeware	25cm (10in) square tin	25cm (10in) square tin	1 litre (2pt/5 cup) & 750ml (1 ¼ pt/3 cup) ovenproof bowls (¾ fill each bowl)
Self-raising flour	315g (10oz/2 ½ cups)	375g (12oz/3 cups)	315g (10oz/2 ½ cups)
Plain (all-purpose) flour	155g (5oz/1 ¼ cups)	185g (6oz/1 ½ cups)	155g (5oz/1 ¼ cups)
Butter or soft margarine	315g (10oz/1 ¼ cups)	375g (12oz/1 ½ cups)	315g (10oz/1 ¼ cups)
Caster (superfine) sugar	315g (10oz/1 ¼ cups)	375g (12oz/1 ½ cups)	315g (10oz/1 ¼ cups)
Eggs (large)	5	6	5
Baking time	45 mins	1 hour	1 ½ hours (large) 1 hour (small)

Cake designs	Popeye (page 46)	Noddy (page 66)	Budgie The Little Helicopter (page 38)
Bakeware	20cm (8in) round tin	23x13cm (9x5in) oblong tin	two 1 litre (2pt/5cup) ovenproof bowls
Self-raising flour	250g (8oz/2 cups)	315g (10oz/2 ½ cups)	250g (8oz/2 cups)
Plain (all-purpose) flour	125g (4oz/1 cup)	155g (5oz/1 ¼ cups)	125g (4oz/1 cup)
Butter or soft margarine	250g (8oz/1 cup)	315g (10oz/1 ¼ cups)	250g (8oz/1 cup)
Caster (superfine) sugar	250g (8oz/1 cup)	315g (10oz/1 ¼ cups)	250g (8oz/1 cup)
Eggs (large)	4	5	4
Baking time	50 mins	1 hour	1 hour

Where's Wally? (page 70)	Old Bear (page 58)	Betty Boop (page 15)	Spot (page 55)
two 1 litre (2pt/5 cup) ovenproof bowls or spherical tin	20cm (8in) square tin	20cm (8in) heart tin	18cm (7in) square tin
315g (10oz/2 ½ cups)	315g (10oz/2 ½ cups)	250g (8oz/2 cups)	250g (8oz/2 cups)
155g (5oz/1 ¼ cups)	155g (5oz/1 ¼ cups)	125g (4oz/1 cup)	125g (4oz/1 cup)
315g (10oz/1 ¼ cups)	315g (10oz/1 ¼ cups)	250g (8oz/1 cup)	250g (8oz/1 cup)
315g (10oz/1 ¼ cups)	315g (10oz/1 ¼ cups)	250g (8oz/1 cup)	250g (8oz/1 cup)
5	5	4	4
1 ¼ hours	1 hour	50 mins	50 mins

Thomas the Tank Engine (page 50)	Postman Pat (page 34)	Mr. Men (page 80)	Peter Rabbit & Friends (page 76)
30x20cm (12x8in) oblong tin	18cm (7in) square tin	20cm (8in) square tin	20cm (8in) hexagonal tin
375g (12oz/3 cups)	315g (10oz/2 ½ cups)	440g (14oz/3 ½ cups)	315g (10oz/2 ½ cups)
185g (6oz/1 ½ cups)	155g (5oz/1 ¼ cups)	220g (7oz/1¾ cups)	155g (5oz/1 ¼ cups)
375g (12oz/1 ½ cups)	315g (10oz/1 ¼ cups)	440g (14oz/1¾ cups)	315g (10oz/1 ¼ cups)
375g (12oz/1 ½ cups)	315g (10oz/1 ¼ cups)	440g (14oz/1¾ cups)	315g (10oz/1 ¼ cups)
6	5	7	5
1 hour	1 hour	1 ½ hours	1 hour

Hints & Tips

★ If your cake has to be cut into shapes, store it in an airtight container for at least 6 hours before use to allow the texture to settle.

★ After the buttercream is spread on the surface of the cake, it might begin to set before you apply the sugarpaste (rolled fondant). If so, simply rework the buttercream with a knife or apply a little more.

★ A sharp serrated knife is best for cake cutting and trimming, but a sharp plain-edged knife is best for cutting paste. To avoid paste 'pulling', do not draw the knife through the paste, but cut cleanly downwards. ▲

★ Wear plastic gloves when kneading the colours into paste as the food colouring might stain your hands.

★ Use icing (confectioners') sugar when rolling out paste and keep moving the paste around to prevent sticking. ▼

★ When a large piece of sugarpaste (rolled fondant) is rolled out, lift by folding over the rolling pin. This will make it easier to position. ▲

★ To avoid undue mess and to regulate amounts, apply food colouring to all icing and modelling pastes using cocktail sticks (toothpicks).

★ Roll the sugarpaste (rolled fondant) to a thickness of 3–4mm (⅛ inch) unless otherwise stated.

★ You might wish to remove the piece of sugarpaste from the area of cake board on which the cake will sit. Because the cake is moist, the sugarpaste underneath has a tendency to become slightly sticky.

★ When the sugarpaste is dry, polish the surface with your hands to remove excess icing (confectioners') sugar and to give a sheen.

★ Keep coloured icings separate as colours may bleed into others when stored.

★ To obtain a smooth surface on sugarpaste, rub gently with a cake smoother, moving it in a circular motion. ▼

★ Sugarpaste-covered cake boards are best left to dry for 12 hours before use. If the cake board is needed before, add ½ teaspoon of gum tragacanth or similar additive to the sugarpaste so the board will dry harder much quicker. ▲

★ Knead the paste until warm and pliable before use.

★ Always store paste icing in an air-tight container and/or polythene bags.

★ Thoroughly remove excess icing (confectioners') sugar from the surface of dried paste before attempting any painting or drawing, as the colours might spread.

★ Food colourings can be diluted with either clear alcohol (gin or vodka) or cool boiled water for painting. Use clear alcohol in preference as this evaporates more quickly. ▼

★ When choosing ribbon for the cake board banding, remember you need a slightly thicker width if you cover the cake board with sugarpaste (rolled fondant). ▲

★ Store the finished cake in a cardboard box in a warm dry room. NEVER store in the refrigerator; the atmosphere is damp and the cake will spoil.

★ To help hold modelled heads in place, push a sugar stick (see page 13) or length of raw dried spaghetti down into each body, then gently push on the heads.

★ Paint scenes and figures first and leave to dry before positioning on the cake and boards. For tips on achieving painting effects, see pages 11–13.

★ Food colouring pens are ideal for adding small details, and are easier to handle than a paintbrush. ▼

Templates

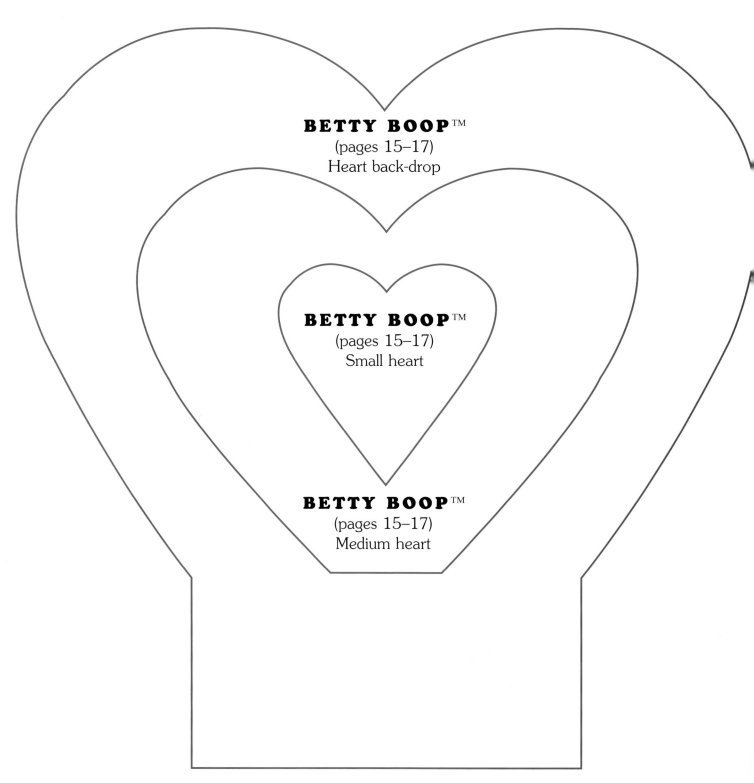

BETTY BOOP™
(pages 15–17)
Heart back-drop

BETTY BOOP™
(pages 15–17)
Small heart

BETTY BOOP™
(pages 15–17)
Medium heart

SOOTY™
(pages 18–21)
Star

PEANUTS™
(pages 26–28)
Snoopy's ear (make 2)

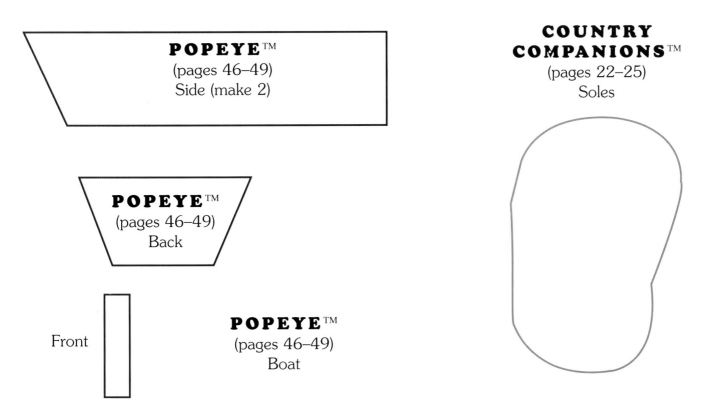

POPEYE™
(pages 46–49)
Side (make 2)

**COUNTRY
COMPANIONS**™
(pages 22–25)
Soles

POPEYE™
(pages 46–49)
Back

Front

POPEYE™
(pages 46–49)
Boat

NODDY™
(pages 66–69)
Soft–top

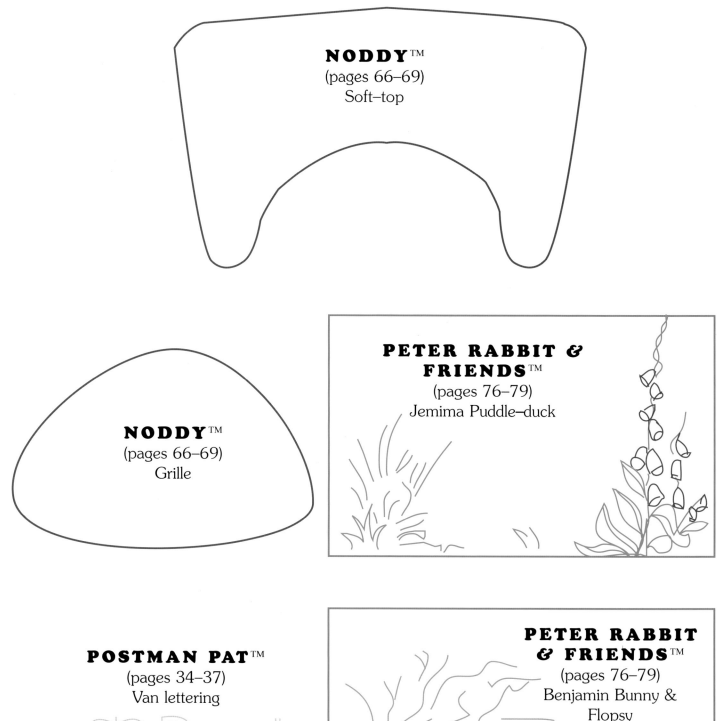

NODDY™
(pages 66–69)
Grille

PETER RABBIT &
FRIENDS™
(pages 76–79)
Jemima Puddle–duck

POSTMAN PAT™
(pages 34–37)
Van lettering

PETER RABBIT
& FRIENDS™
(pages 76–79)
Benjamin Bunny &
Flopsy

FOREVER FRIENDS™
(pages 42–45)
Decoration guides

Roses   Patterns

PETER RABBIT
& FRIENDS™
(pages 76–79)
Mrs Tittlemouse

THOMAS THE
TANK ENGINE
(pages 50–54)

PETER RABBIT
& FRIENDS™
(pages 76–79)
Jeremy Fisher

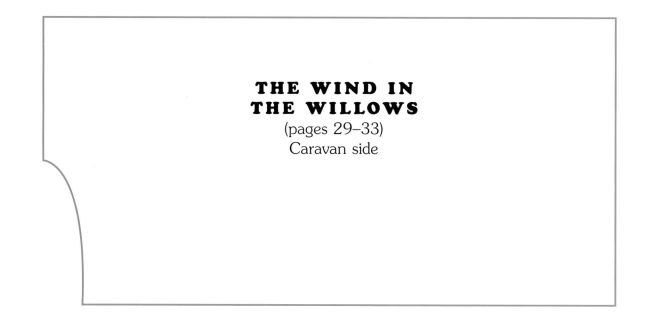

**THE WIND IN
THE WILLOWS**
(pages 29–33)
Caravan side

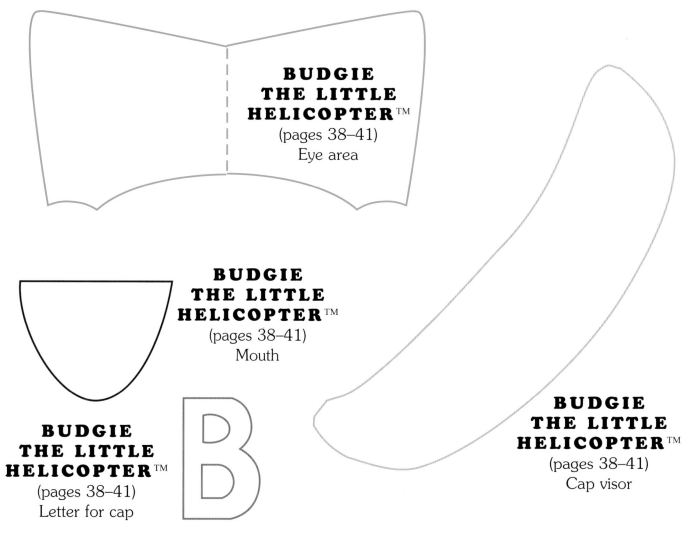

**BUDGIE
THE LITTLE
HELICOPTER**™
(pages 38–41)
Eye area

**BUDGIE
THE LITTLE
HELICOPTER**™
(pages 38–41)
Mouth

**BUDGIE
THE LITTLE
HELICOPTER**™
(pages 38–41)
Cap visor

**BUDGIE
THE LITTLE
HELICOPTER**™
(pages 38–41)
Letter for cap

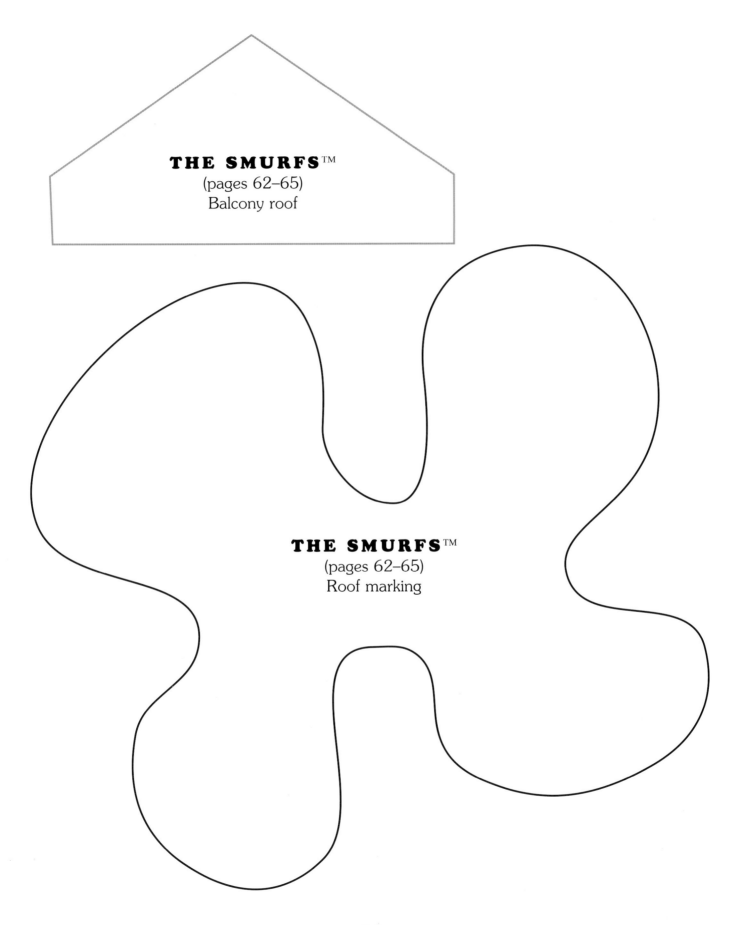

THE SMURFS™
(pages 62–65)
Balcony roof

THE SMURFS™
(pages 62–65)
Roof marking

Index

ACKNOWLEDGEMENTS

The author would like to thank the following:
Barbara Croxford, a really special lady who deserves a big thankyou for all her help, patience and understanding through what was a long, frustrating and nail-biting effort to put this book together.

All the copyright holders who said YES!

My husband Paul, for the miles and miles of driving, for lugging boxes for me, and for all his patience and support.

Mum and Dad for being on 'call'.

My children, Lewis, Laura and Shaun, for having a ready supply of toys, comics, stickers and books to help me design all the cakes. Rhys, Daniel, Sarah and Leanne for supplying even more.

The author and publishers would also like to thank the following suppliers:

Anniversary House (Cake Decorations) Ltd.
Unit 5,
Roundways,
Elliott Road,
Bournemouth,
Hants. BH11 8JJ

Cake Art Ltd.
Venture Way,
Crown Estate,
Priorswood,
Taunton,
Somerset TA2 8DE

Guy, Paul and Co. Ltd.
Unit B4,
Foundry Way,
Little End Road,
Eaton Socon,
Cambs. PE19 3JH

J. F. Renshaw Ltd.
Crown Street,
Liverpool L8 7RF

Squires Kitchen
Squires House,
3 Waverley Lane,
Farnham,
Surrey GU9 8BB